THE CLASSROOM
and
THE CELL

THE CLASSROOM
—— and ——
THE CELL

CONVERSATIONS ON
BLACK LIFE IN AMERICA

Mumia Abu-Jamal & Marc Lamont Hill

Progressive Black Publishing Since 1967

Third World Press
Chicago

Third World Press
Publishers since 1967
Chicago

© 2014 by Mumia Abu-Jamal and Marc Lamont Hill

First Edition
Printed in the United States of America

Library of Congress Control Number: 2011940558

ISBN 13: 978-0-88378-337-5

16 15 14 13 12 11   6 5 4 3 2 1

To those who love us and whom we love...

To those churning in an unloving world and burning
to fulfill their purpose...

To those in cages of steel, brick, fear or hatred...

To those who come after us, whose work it will be to undo our messes
and create a world where life is more precious than profit...

You have our undying love, gratitude and solidarity

Mumia Abu-Jamal
Marc Lamont Hill

Contents

Introduction

How does a work like this come to be?

It is not by mere chance, yet who can deny that chance played a part?

Two men, separated by class, social standing and generations—not to mention brick, steel and concrete—come together.

One is not merely free but decidedly privileged, an academic ensconced in one of the nation's premier Ivy League universities. The other, is not simply un-free, but caged *en extremis*, on death row, in one of the country's most infamous prisons.

One is living by the professorial adage "publish or perish." The other is facing the very real possibility of publishing *and* perishing.

Two men who weren't supposed to know each other.

Yet somehow, we not only managed to find one another, but to forge a deep friendship, brotherhood and love. This book, *The Classroom and the Cell: Conversations on Black Life in America*, is one of the many fruits of that bond.

Through countless phone calls, letters and visits over the past few years, we have plumbed themes of commonality. Both of us are Black men from North Philadelphia, lifelong activists and fathers. We are both a mere three generations from slavery, living in an era more remarkable than our forbearers could ever have dreamed.

While each of us marvels at the ascendance of a Black man to the presidency of the United States, we are sobered by the reality that Black men represent the lowest percentile of college students, as well as the highest percentage of state and federal prisoners.

And yet, this is not a work of "woe-is-us" but rather the rumination of two reasonable men, observing, analyzing and contemplating this rich and rare moment in modern American history.

Both of us are serious readers, and we've both earned graduate degrees; the caged, a masters in the humanities; the uncaged a doctorate in the social sciences. Both of us are award-winning authors who have penned works examining this era in the nation's life. Yet, this is not a traditional academic treatise.

Instead, we have decided to converse, in the spirit of, and with inspiration from Margaret Mead and James Baldwin's provocative 1971 book, *A Rap on Race,* and bell hooks and Cornel West's evocative *Breaking Bread*, which came out in 1991. Like them, we have decided to use dialogue as a method of inquiry, cultural criticism, social analysis and, toughest of all, self-examination.

Through our conversations, we wrestle with some of the most pressing questions within the Black community: How do we make sense of Black prosperity in the midst of Black misery? What does it mean to be Black, alive, conscious and resistant in the 21st century? How can we re-imagine the two major spaces that impact Black life—the classroom and the prison cell?

The professor and the prisoner try to answer these questions, and many more, with coherence, sincerity, and, yes, *hope*. Hope that this young century will be better to our people than the last one; hope that we will witness the fruition of long-claimed promises of full citizenship and recognized humanity; hope that we can love ourselves and each other into new levels of joy and freedom.

Ona Move,

M.A.J. (June, 2011)
SCI Greene Prison
Waynesburg, PA

M.L.H. (June, 2011)
Columbia University
New York, NY

CHAPTER 1

Who Am I? Whose Am I?

Because of the nature of our work, each of us is extremely guarded. This is reflected in our writing, which covers many topics but rarely explores our own lives and feelings. At the prodding of our faithful editor, asha bandele, we committed to letting our guards down (a bit!) and connecting the ideas in this book to our own personal narratives. For both of us, this was a challenging but ultimately rewarding experience. In this opening chapter, we wrestle with two seemingly straightforward questions: Who am I? *and* Whose am I? *In answering these questions, we trace the roots and routes of our labor, spotlighting the people, events, traditions and organizations that inform our work and shape our identities.*

Marc: Before meeting you, one of the things I noticed about you is how guarded you are in your writing. You share a little bit in your first book, *Live from Death Row*, but generally you don't talk a lot about yourself. Is that a deliberate decision?

Mumia: It is. After all, it's about the work, you know? It's more important than me. I come from a movement that inculcated in me a real sense of community and collective consciousness, so it was never about me. In one of his first books, Huey P. Newton said, "I am we." In African society, the very idea of an individual is alien. You are a member of a clan, a member of a community. The idea of "nations" is relatively new, and you see how well we're doing with that!

Marc: Right! The flip of that, though, is important, too. The work that we do—our writing, research, speeches and political commitments—leaves hints about our desires, beliefs and fears. No matter how hard we try to hide them, we constantly reveal pieces of ourselves to the world. That's why I think it's so important that we explicitly and transparently reflect on our own narratives. It helps people understand the baggage that we bring to the table and it makes our work more honest. It helps us to understand ourselves better, too. This isn't just true for writers and activists; it's a human thing. We all have to constantly wrestle with that existential question, "Who am I?"

Mumia: I agree with you, at least from the perspective of asking that question as a writer, and as someone who, despite this dogged captivity, has a public life.

Marc: With that in mind, who are you?

Mumia: Well, that's a profound question. It depends, of course, on the questioner. I'm not the same person to a former comrade as I am to my grandchild. I am a thinker, writer, activist, creative being, man, dad, husband, grandpop and son. But just to keep it simple: I'm a free Black man living in captivity. That's who I am.

You're in prison, but somehow still free, while I'm out here feeling profoundly UN-FREE.

Marc: "A free Black man living in captivity." That's powerful and complex, man. Negotiating freedom and unfreedom at the same time.

Mumia: Well, I ain't trying to say nothing slick about myself. I think a good percentage of Black men can answer that question the same way, or at least halfway, 'cause we in captivity in this country. We still ain't free. I'll never forget the words of Harriet Tubman, when everybody was praising her for freeing so many Black folks. She said, "I could've freed a thousand more if only they knew they were slaves." That idea is still true today. We are the freest un-free people in the world.

Marc: When you use the word "free," what do you mean? Why do you see yourself as free?

Mumia: Because I say what's in my heart. I know a whole lot of Black men who don't have that freedom. They can think something, they can feel it, they can go to church and pray about it, but they can't say it because they're afraid of losing their job. They're afraid of losing their status. You dig what I'm saying?

Marc: No doubt. I work in media, politics and academia and in all three spaces I'm surrounded by people who won't say what they really feel, who won't tell their truths, because they're afraid of the repercussions.

Mumia: So how free are you?

Marc: That's a hell of a question. When I think about myself, all sorts of words come to mind. Depending on the situation, I would say things like "father," "activist," "writer" or "professor." But "free" is one thing I wouldn't say for myself. In fact, I would describe you as being far freer than me. I can't avoid seeing the irony that you're in prison but somehow still free, while I'm out here feeling profoundly un-free.

Mumia: When you talk about your lack of freedom, you're talking about the golden chains that are on you. They're pretty as a muthafucka, but they're still chains. I think it's interesting that our people, of all the people in the world, chose chains as a fashion accessory.

Marc: Crazy right? And we call our cars "whips!"

Mumia: Damn! Whips and chains. *That* ain't a Freudian slip. Ain't no such thing! We're not even free in our language. You dig what I'm saying?

Marc: No doubt.

Mumia: Frederick Douglass said that of all people, Black people worshipped freedom. Freedom was on our tongues, in our dreams, in our churches, everywhere 'cause we knew what it meant not to have it. Nevertheless, we still ain't free. Some of the least free people in this country are members of the Black bourgeoisie because they know better. Political leaders have certain shit they cannot say because they'll catch it. Black athletes might make $20, $30, $40 million a year, but...

Marc: But they can't say shit—well other than Muhammad Ali, who was the last prominent athlete who spoke out against social injustice. And who was the last powerful politician who took a real risk? There are some, but not many.

Mumia: Right. So you're making a hell of a paycheck, but how free are you?

Marc: And, for me, that feeling of being un-free doesn't just come from a fear of speaking my truths or an anxiety about being unpopular. In many ways, I've learned to overcome those fears. Hell, if I hadn't already, doing a book with you would be a crash course for sure!

Mumia: You ain't lyin'!

Marc: But to some degree, I feel un-free because I'm still encumbered by the very things that I'm critiquing in my work: consumerism, patriarchy even White supremacy. I'm trying to close the gap between theory and practice, between public and private, between who I am and who I want to be. I'm trying to heal, man. That requires lots of struggle, lots of thinking and lots of reflection. Not to mention, lots of therapy. It's hard work! But I'm not healed and I'm not whole and that reality gives me a lingering sense of un-freedom. That feeling is as central to my identity as anything else.

Mumia: In truth, none of us are whole, as in finished, for we are all beings who are still in the process of becoming. We are trying to live in the midst of struggle against forces that try, daily, to confine, constrain and restrict our being. In a sense, these forces are as powerful, relentless and invisible as gravity—there, but not there, dig me? So we seek to heal in a place that is profoundly unhealthy. Consumerism, patriarchy, White supremacy and acquisitiveness are things that grip us all. We're all fish swimming in that proverbial Dead Sea of materialism, seeking fresh water where we can wash our gills.

Marc: And I think everyone struggles with these feelings, even those who benefit from the un-freedom of others. No one is free until everyone is free. White people can never be free as long as White supremacy exists. Men can never be free as long as patriarchy exists. Straight people can never be free as long as homophobia exists. That's not just some liberal cliché, it's a profound truth that sits in our souls. Even if we ignore or suppress it, we are still haunted by our role in the unmerited suffering of others. It becomes part of who we are.

I'm trying to close the gap between who I am and who I WANT to be.

Mumia: Our challenge, it seems to me, is to be or become sensitive, feeling and loving beings who seek to better the environment into which we were born. Speaking of liberal clichés, we must "make it better." And it is that very doing that becomes part of our being, for we join in our hearts, minds, mouths and then our bodies in the struggles of those unfree amongst us. In a real sense, we become them. I think that was the life message of folks like Martin Luther King, Jr. and Malcolm X, and why we remember and revere them. We felt them. Martin gave up the ghost for *garbage men* in Memphis. Malcolm reached out to brothers in the Arab and African worlds and became a part of them. In many ways, they redefined who "we" were and became a part of us through their impact on our lives and consciousness.

Marc: The other word you used was "Black." What does Blackness mean to you and why is it so central to your identity?

Mumia: Part of the reason I use "Black" as opposed to other terms is because we fought hard in the '60s and '70s to use that word. We used it because it was the plainest statement of who we were. We couldn't talk about being American or even African-Americans living in the United States when we had none of the rights of Americans and very few of us knew anything fundamental about Africa.

Marc: Right.

Mumia: We were certainly African, genetically and by blood. But we were lost when it came to language and culture and all those kinds of things. When you think of the most organized Black community of that era, The Nation of Islam, they didn't call themselves Africans. They said "Asiatic." So while our generation certainly looked to the African continent, people and freedom struggles for inspiration, we understood that our struggle here was different.

Marc: How important, then, was it for you to take on an African name? How does being "Mumia Abu-Jamal" affect how you assert who you are in the world? How is that different than being "Wesley Cook," the man with the name you were given at birth?

Mumia: For me, it has cultural and temporal relevance. When I was a teenager studying Swahili in high school—

Marc: —Swahili in high school?

Mumia: Yep! Now ain't that the '60s? Our teacher, a brother from Kenya, gave the whole class African names to facilitate language usage and comfort with these foreign sounds. Now, that experience wasn't unique to that class. I recall the teacher in my junior high Spanish class giving us Spanish names. She gave me the name Vicente because it was the closest thing to Wesley. Now, our Swahili teacher assigned names without respect to our English names. I remember asking him what Mumia meant and he said

Slaves weren't brought to America. PEOPLE were.

"paramount prince." Well that sounded cool to me! I learned years later that Mumia was an anti-colonial fighter against British settlers in Kenya, and I believe Mau Mau. Years later, when my first child was born, I took the honorific "Abu" ("father of") Jamal. One funny thing: When he first wrote the names of the fellows on the blackboard, I copied it down as "Mumsia." Boy, that was a mouthful!

Being in PRISON for one's political beliefs and resistance was as normal as pancakes for breakfast.

Marc: Now, you're also inside of a prison, sitting on death row. How does that reality inform how you see yourself in the world?

Mumia: Well, that's why I used the term "captivity." Terms like "inmate" or "prisoner" are just labels we put on people. Even the most enlightened history books about our people refer to us as "slaves." We weren't slaves; we were *enslaved*. We were captive.

Marc: That's an important point. Words like "slave" allow our humanity to be stripped away. Slaves weren't brought to America. *People* were. While we can get people to accept that notion, at least theoretically, it's harder for some of us to see the fundamental humanity of brothers and sisters in prison, much less death row. Your use of the term "captive" speaks not only to your refusal to lose sight of your own humanity, but also to the fundamental unjustness of your incarceration. How do you make sense of your particular struggle with captivity?

Mumia: You must understand that I grew up in a reality that did not make this remarkable or out of the ordinary. When I joined the Black Panther Party, Huey P. Newton was in prison, Angela Y. Davis was imprisoned shortly thereafter, and the New York Panther 21 were in prison and facing zillions of years. So being in prison for one's political beliefs and resistance was as normal as pancakes for breakfast.

Marc: Over the past 30 years, you have become more than just a respected writer and cause célèbre. You have also become an international symbol of social injustice and you've emerged as one of the nation's leading public intellectuals. What do those two roles mean to you?

Mumia: In some ways, I feel like it won't get said if I don't say it. That's probably why my wife tells me to shut up! I just think the political class has become so compromised that they have little to say to the poor, except "take it" or "shut up." I write because I'm a writer and I'm perhaps read so widely because so many folks ain't really hitting on the themes that I do. As far as being one of the leading public intellectuals? That means somebody else ain't doin' they job, huh? I think in many ways I'm still just the scribe I was as a teenager, writing and fighting. Instead of using a mimeograph machine, I'm using other mediums. But the class divide is so corrosive and treacherous that I feel driven to write the way I do. But you're also described as a public intellectual, Marc. As a matter of fact, that title is attached to people like you more often than it is to people like me. Is it something you value?

Marc: Honestly, I don't really value it at all anymore. I used to call myself a public intellectual, but I've come to dislike it as a way to describe who I am and what I do. To me a true public intellectual is someone who, by profession or by practice, links their intellectual engagement to spaces and places beyond the university. In that sense, the best examples of public intellectuals aren't college professors with lucrative TV or book deals, but folk like James Baldwin, Paulo Freire, Grace Lee Boggs and Sonia Sanchez. I'm inclined to use the term to describe those folk because it places a spotlight on their deep intellectual gifts. Too often, the intellectual ability of folk who work outside of the university, or whose work isn't traditionally academic, gets dismissed or understated. That's why I call you a public intellectual without hesitation. Your work is deeply intellectual and has made a powerful intervention into so many critical public conversations. More importantly, you've helped to expose the world to a long and deep tradition of prison intellectuals who have cried out from dungeons all around the world.

Mumia: I appreciate that, bro, but I think you're selling yourself short. You're doing serious work out there in the world, too. If anybody is a public intellectual, it's a cat like you.

Marc: That means a lot coming from you, big bro. I'm definitely trying to do my part to link my intellectual work to real world issues. Some days I do it better than others. But for those of us in the academy, the term "public intellectual" now speaks more to the "public" part than the "intellectual" part. It no longer refers to those of us who do activist work, but to those who have become intellectual celebrities.

Mumia: I agree. And, for sure, there are some folk who are called public intellectuals who haven't done anything but fill their pockets and increase their visibility. But that ain't you.

Marc: No doubt, but those folk you mention have become the model! Look, I've been working in the drug policy reform movement for more than a decade. I've been doing grassroots activism since I was a kid. I'm currently working within the prison abolition movement. Still, nobody called me a public intellectual until I was on national television. That, to me, speaks to a fundamental problem with how we understand the "public," as well as where we think serious intellectual work happens. That's why I prefer the title of "activist intellectual" or "activist scholar" to describe folks like me. It keeps us honest.

Mumia: I hear you. At the same time, though, you have become somewhat of a celebrity. You have your own TV show, you've been a regular cable news pundit, and you have a pretty big presence in national conversations. You do get some personal benefit from the work you do in the mainstream public, right? Even if you don't use that title, it isn't any less true.

Marc: No doubt. But I don't think that fame necessarily makes a person "public" any more than a Ph.D. automatically makes them an "intellectual." For me, there are multiple publics that include churches, unions, prisons and grassroots organizations. I tend to measure my public engagement based on my level of involvement with those folk, not by a Nielsen box. At the same time, I don't pretend that I'm not in those other spaces too. That's why I try to use the media in strategic and principled ways, to advance a cause of justice, rather than purely as a vehicle for my own personal advancement. More importantly, I try to keep track of the many times that I fall short, as well as the irreconcilable contradictions between my politics and my presence in some of these places. It's a constant struggle. Most days, I think I make good decisions. But some days, I don't.

Mumia: You mentioned that you were an activist as a kid. How did you get so involved at such a young age?

Marc: My family asks me that question all the time! They think I'm like an alien or something because nobody in my house was an activist, or even that political. I did, however, grow up surrounded by a bunch of Black institutions that helped me craft an activist disposition pretty early on in my life.

Mumia: What kinds of institutions?

Marc: The first institution was my home. I grew up in North and West Philly in the '80s. We lived in North Philly for the first half of my childhood before eventually moving to West Philly. I was living in one of the poorest and most violent neighborhoods in the city despite the fact that my mom and dad could afford to move out. Although my parents weren't activists, or even political, their decision to stay in the neighborhood influenced me more than just about anything else. They believed that staying mattered. They believed that the way to protect and advance our communities was to stay and build rather than to leave for so-called greener pastures. They instilled in me a commitment to developing and supporting our communities from the inside rather than as drive-by philanthropists. They also modeled an effortless love for Black people that was never discussed but always apparent. Also, growing up in the 'hood, I had access to all sorts of Black people: welfare mothers, union workers, preachers, teachers, pimps, cops, stick-up boys, crack addicts and Black revolutionaries. Poor people have never been caricatures or sociological subjects to me. They've been my neighbors, friends and family. These experiences were key in shaping my activism. I don't romanticize poverty, nor do I uncritically celebrate Black culture. My childhood allowed me to bear witness to the fundamental humanity of everyday Black people, a humanity that has been dishonored and denied by the hellish conditions in which we've been placed. How about you? What pushed you toward activism so early?

Mumia: My old man, a country guy, always brought me books. He brought his other boys baseball gloves, bats and toys, but he brought me books. And I read them. Very few were "Black books," but he encouraged my reading so I read widely. Once, an older sister in the neighborhood named Audrey gave me two things to read: *Ramparts* magazine, which had a big article on Eldridge Cleaver, and a copy of *The Black Panther* newspaper. I read both over and over and over. I couldn't believe it! To say I was captivated was an understatement; I was blown away. Was the idea of being an intellectual instilled in you early?

Marc: No, I wouldn't say that. The idea of being an intellectual, as a profession, is in many ways a bourgeois notion. For most Black folk, including my parents, the idea of reading and writing for a living was unimaginable. My parents did, however, emphasize the importance of education very early in my life. My mother, who was a schoolteacher, read to me as a baby and taught me to read by the time I was 3 or 4. I quickly developed a sense that literacy was an important pathway into the world. I was a voracious reader and eventually stumbled into Black nationalist literature. From that point forward, I was hooked!

Mumia: I read voraciously too, but hardcore nationalist literature came later. When I joined the Black Panther Party we read Mao, Che, Nkrumah and Fanon, among others.

Marc: The first book that moved me was *The Autobiography of Malcolm X*. It completely changed my orientation to the world. After reading it, I came to believe that reading and writing could change, or even save our lives. The book lit a fire inside of me. When I wasn't playing basketball, I was hanging out at Hakim's Bookstore on 52nd Street and Basic Black Books in the Gallery mall. I devoured everything those stores offered. Books like *The*

Isis Papers, Behold a Pale Horse and *Message to the Black Man in America* provided me with an out-of-school education that sent me down a lifelong path of self-exploration and racial identity development. I also began to develop a radical politic that I'm still refining and reshaping to this day. The other book that changed my life was *Assata*, which I read years later. Hearing the story of Assata Shakur, the political revolutionary wrongfully convicted of murder, opened my eyes to a more grounded form of radical politics. It also opened my eyes to the plight of political prisoners in America. Until then, I never realized how many people were railroaded by our government because of their political beliefs and affiliations. Her story inspired me to become a writer and an anti-prison activist. Lots of books have had powerful effects on me, but nothing like Assata's and Malcolm's. Without a drop of hyperbole I can say that those books saved my life.

Mumia: The book that knocked me out was Eldridge [Cleaver's] *Soul on Ice*. Of course, Eldridge is now understood in a very different way, in terms of his politics and stances on women. But at that time I was hooked on his mind and his writing style. After that it was *The Wretched of the Earth* by Frantz Fanon, the Algerian revolutionary from Martinique. It was a difficult book, but it gave me an international perspective. My chapter of the Party used to actually meet at a bookstore downtown before we ever got an office. The storeowner was cool enough to let us read, study and hang there. They had whole sections on Africa, Asia and Vietnam. You name it, and we probably read it!

Marc: Reading so much made me interested in a bunch of organizations. Early on, I was captivated by the Nation of Islam, the Nation of Gods and Earths (Five Percenters) and the Ansaaru Allah communities, all of which were hugely influential in cities like Philadelphia, New York, Chicago and Detroit. As a teenager, I saw Islam as a pathway to freedom for Black people. I saw leaders like Imam Isa, Louis Farrakhan and Khalid Muhammad as role models. As I got older, though, I developed sharp disagreements with each of them. After joining the Ansaars, I became disillusioned by Imam Isa's deep immorality and problematic doctrine. I also disagreed with Minister Farrakhan's economic and gender politics. Although I admired and respected him deeply, and I continue to do so today, I came to see his politics as extremely conservative and politically counterproductive. I also struggled with the Nation of Islam's version of Islam, which always felt more Christian-centered than Islamic. I very much loved and admired Khalid Muhammad, who I met as a teenager while working with a grassroots nationalist organization in Philadelphia called United for Success. I was particularly moved by his tireless love of Black people and his strong grassroots commitment. He was extremely kind and gentle—nothing like the firebrand who was broadcast on national television. Every time we saw each other I learned a great deal and I always walked away feeling reenergized and motivated to struggle for justice. Still, I never felt comfortable with his views about Whites and Jews, which cast them as naturally and inalterably evil. Although I've always had a strong critique of White people in America, I refuse to deny the fundamental humanity and possibilities of any racial or ethnic group as a biological fact. As I got older, I became completely disillusioned with the religious organizations and grew more interested in political movements. You, on the other hand, seemed to start out in political organizations. You helped start a branch of the Black Panthers in Philly when you were 15 years old. How did that happen? What sparked you?

Mumia: Well, I was tall, a little thick, and I had a moustache at 14. Most of the guys didn't know I was that young. When we got together and rapped, I would contribute like the older guys 'cause I too had read the *Black Panther* newspaper, *The Wretched of the Earth*, etcetera. Also, in the summer of 1968 when I was 14, the cops beat me up for protesting a pro-George Wallace rally. It was a revolutionary time and everybody was militant. Believe it or not, it really wasn't remarkable.

Marc: Did your work with the Panthers inspire you to become a journalist?

Mumia: Yes. I got into reporting and writing because of my membership in the Black Panther Party. I worked in the Ministry of Information in three states, writing leaflets, sending reports to the national office that would often turn up in the newspaper, and working on that very paper several years later. I was also influenced by the writings and tapes of Huey P. Newton and Eldridge Cleaver. You know, in many ways the conflict between Huey and Eldridge reminded me of the one between Elijah Muhammad and Malcolm X. Huey was quite a poor public speaker while Eldridge was a natural-born speaker. I think that came to be a bone of contention between the two men. But boy, could they write! Huey was brilliant and so was Eldridge! Also, Zayd Malik Shakur was my mentor. When I was working out of the Bronx Ministry office, Zayd taught me a great deal.

Marc: Wow. I didn't know you worked with Zayd! Of course, I only know him from Assata Shakur's autobiography, as police murdered him on May 2, 1973, the night Assata was unjustly arrested on the New Jersey Turnpike.

Mumia: Yeah, we worked out of the same office in the Bronx, which was really the Ministry of Information not only for the New York state branches but, ultimately, for the whole East Coast. Zayd was deputy minister of information. I worked there putting together leaflets, booklets, brochures—whatever was needed. He was a beautiful dude. If you never knew him, you missed a brilliant life and light. He was unlike a lot of the ultra-macho brothers in the Party. This cat was a very witty, urbane, brilliantly well-read and a gentle soul. I'm 14, 15 years old, and he's reciting Khalil Gibran's *The Prophet* from memory, talking about its beauty. I'm like, *Damn*. You know what I mean?

Marc: I do.

Mumia: Those were the kind of cats I saw. And, you know, sisters really impacted me too. I had the pleasure and the honor of really being with sisters like Safiya Bukhari, who was a real firecracker, you hear me? She was this short but intense woman who worked harder than everybody else. And woe unto the Panther who didn't hustle! She made sure work got done. I also learned from Judi Douglas, who was the editor of the national newspaper when I was out there in California. She wasn't just the boss or the editor; she took the time to teach and critique. In her gentle, Southern voice, she'd help you become a better, clearer writer. These sisters around me were just astonishing. You never saw more hardworking people in your life. So I think about those people who formed my consciousness at a very early age and who showed me a kind of love and sacrifice for their people that most can't imagine. You know, when you think of the Black Panther Party, you think of Huey, Eldridge or maybe the famous poster. But it was the sisters who really held it together. They opened the offices, they ran the breakfast program and they cracked the whip when they had to. I know Safiya certainly cracked a whip on my ass when I was working up in New York! These were just astonishing people. They were my teachers.

Marc: At some point did you leave the party formally, or did you just transition into other stuff?

Mumia: I did leave the party, at the beginning of the struggle between the East and West Coasts. It was so painful to see brothers fighting each other that it broke my heart. Now I look back and see that most of that was engineered by the government. But it was also ego that allowed our leading members to fall into the State's trap. If brothers could've just talked to each other and left their egos outside the door, a lot of the issues could've been washed away.

Marc: That's real, man. I was born in December '78 so my experience wasn't with the Panthers, but with Muslim organizations in Philly. The Ansaars were fighting the Nation of Islam; the Nation was fighting the Sunnis. And, of course, there were vicious and bloody wars with Hanafi brothers and sisters, which led to the loss of many lives.

Mumia: Oh yes. Oh yes.

Marc: I was trying to figure out where to go and what to join. To some extent I felt like I was choosing between rival gangs rather than organizations trying to make a community better.

Mumia: It's remarkable that, in all those movements, we were so busy fighting each other that we forgot to fight the oppressor.

Marc: Right! Right! Like you with the Panthers, I got disillusioned because we were talking about everything except freeing ourselves. It became about individuals and not about the movement.

Mumia: We misused our power. We misled the people. That's one of the reasons I wrote *We Want Freedom*. I want us to learn from our errors. The new generation can look at us and say, "We ain't going out this way." We have to do this because our people are still in pain.

Marc: In addition to the Panthers, you are also known for your connection to MOVE, a naturalist revolutionary organization based in Philadelphia. What was your relationship to it?

Mumia: Well, as you might expect, coming from the Party, my feelings about any organization were so raw that I had no intention in joining anything. So when I first read about MOVE, from the tenor of what I read in the papers—well, I was repulsed. Then, in my work as a local reporter when I ran into them and really talked to them, I found something quite distinct from what I had read. They were, well, people. Warm. Funny. Passionate. And deeply, deeply committed. Years ago I

One of my earliest memories was the 1985 bombing of MOVE. Philadelphia dropped a bomb on a residential block and let the fire burn for half a day.

wrote about the case of Life Africa, a little boy who was beaten out of his mother's arms by the cops. Even though I had no intentions of joining anything, I felt drawn to them because no matter what, they kept right on rumblin' against the system.

Marc: One of my earliest childhood memories was the May 13, 1985 bombing of MOVE. The city of Philadelphia literally dropped a bomb on Osage Avenue—a residential block—and let the fire burn for almost half a day. Sixty one homes were destroyed and countless people were killed or severely wounded. While I don't remember exactly how the tragedy was discussed, I do remember that the members of MOVE were matter-of-factly described in animalistic terms by the mainstream media. The founder, John Africa, was framed as a cult leader. What was your experience with him? How did he affect how you see the world?

Mumia: Well, I learned from personal experience and observation that the news coverage was profoundly biased so why wouldn't that extend to John Africa? I didn't spend a lot of time around him, but my wife and I went to the house on Osage, the one eventually bombed by the cops, a day or two after the federal trial where he and another brother were acquitted. John was calm, sitting on a carpet with a clean white sweatshirt, a pair of jeans and bare feet. There were a few MOVE members there, along with Brother Abdul and a big group of kids playing in the basement, running up and down the stairs. We asked questions and he answered them calmly, in a deep resonant voice. Not pontificating, just explaining. It wasn't preaching. It was a discussion. That's when he said how strong women were. It went something like this: "Women are stronger than men, but you are taught the opposite, that men are the strongest, right?" Abdul and I looked at each other and while we didn't say, "You are wrong," it was clear from our expressions that we didn't buy it. He said, "Well, wouldn't you agree that it takes strong people to be in MOVE, to go through what MOVE goes through?" To that, we had to agree. Then he asked, "What do you see around you?" There were three men: John, Abdul and me. The rest were women and children. He then said, "If it were up to men to give birth, the human race would die quick!" and he laughed, as did we all, 'cause it was funny. But it was also true. He was serious, funny, brilliant and deeply committed. And yes, I saw the animal in his dark, feral eyes. Believe it or not, it exists in all of us, but we let the system use it for others' gain.

Marc: When it's all said and done, how do you want the world to see you? What do you want people to say one hundred years from now when the question is asked, "Who was Mumia Abu-Jamal?"

Mumia: They'll say that he was a man who loved, struggled and resisted for his people. Of course, none of us can truly influence such matters. We just do the best of what we do in the land of the living. That's enough, it seems to me. Thomas Paine, in my mind the greatest so-called founding father, said, "A share in two revolutions is living to same purpose." I've been involved in radical and revolutionary movements since before I could shave. I have made some contribution to the Black freedom movements and other human rights movements. That's not a small thing. But, if I'm just remembered as someone who loved his people, I'm cool with that. How about you? How will Marc Lamont Hill be remembered?

Marc: My sincerest hope is that I'll be remembered as a freedom fighter. Everything else aside, I want to be remembered as someone who fought to make the world a little bit more fair, a little bit more just, and a little bit more livable for others. I also want people to think of

I hope that if I am remembered, it will be because I was someone who loved his people.

me as someone who wrestled with his own deep contradictions and emerged, like you, as a free Black man. If people can say all that, then I lived one hell of a life.

Mumia: And that ain't no small thing either!

Marc: Nope, I guess not.

FOR YOUR LIBRARY

At the end of each chapter we suggest several books that we believe will help inform your understanding of our points of view. The lists are hardly exhaustive. They include works mentioned in chapter or others that most directly informed the conversation. We encourage you to view these small compilations as ever-developing and include your own sources of intellectual and spiritual rigor.

We Want Freedom, Mumia Abu-Jamal

Yurugu, Marimba Ani

The War Before, Safiya Bukhari

Soul on Ice, Eldridge Cleaver

The Narrative of the Life of Frederick Douglass, Frederick Douglass

Wretched of the Earth, Frantz Fanon

Pedagogy of the Oppressed, Paulo Freire

The Prophet, Khalil Gibran

How Capitalism Underdeveloped Black America, Manning Marable

Message to the Black Man in America, Elijah Muhammad

Assata, Assata Shakur

The Isis Papers, Frances Cress Welsing

Blueprint for Black Power, Amos Wilson

The Autobiography of Malcolm X, Malcolm X, with Alex Haley

Quotations from Chairman Mao, by Mao Zedung

CHAPTER 2

Reimagining Race in the Era of Obama

We began our regular conversations about halfway through the historic 2008 presidential election. As each week passed, we became more and more engrossed in the drama of the primary and general elections. Despite the optimistic polling numbers, we both had serious doubts about America's readiness to elect a Black man to the nation's highest office. When Barack Obama won on November 4, 2008, we both felt a strange mix of pride and fear, hope and skepticism. Unlike many Americans, particularly White citizens looking to forget the country's tortured racial history, we fully resisted the idea that the emergence of a Black president signified the dawn of a "post-racial" moment in history. At the same time, we couldn't deny that the Obama presidency occasioned a new moment in America's complicated racial history. Now, in the aftermath of the election, we continue to uncover new layers of meaning regarding President Obama's remarkable victory, White America's post-election response to President Obama's racial identity, the shifting meaning of race in the Obama era, and the unavoidable paradox of having a Black president in the midst of Black suffering.

Marc: When we first started talking, we were in the middle of the 2008 presidential campaign. Despite the sense of inevitability generated by some popular media in the final months, we were both still a little shocked by Obama's historic victory, right?

Mumia: More than a little. You see, long before it became inevitable, it was *impossible*. I think there were many Black folks who never thought they would live to see the day. Not just in my generation, but maybe even quite younger people.

Marc: For sure. A year before the primary election, I remember telling both of my parents that Obama could win the presidency. They laughed at me. Of course, they grew up in the Jim Crow South. Their grandparents were slaves. So for my mom and dad, this didn't become real until the very end.

I didn't want to say what I FEARED, that if he was elected he would be killed.

Mumia: When I was a boy, my father used to tell me, "Wes, one day there's gonna be a Negro president. It won't happen in my lifetime, but it'll happen in yours." He turned out to be right, though it's happened when I'm in my fifties. My father would've been so proud.

Marc: I'm sure he would've been. Just like my parents, who were jumping up in down when it finally happened. I remember being at Fox News doing political analysis on the night of the election. Most of the people looked like they were going to a funeral when they walked into the building, but all the Black people looked like they hit the lottery! Once the final results came in, the Black cameramen and crew shot me secret smiles and thumbs ups. The next day, my brother and I went to Sylvia's restaurant in Harlem and it was buzzing like never before. It felt like all of us were president.

Mumia: I know what you mean. Obviously, I have a certain set of politics and a certain understanding of this country. Still, I couldn't help but feel proud to see that Black man and his family enter the White House. It may not change the political world, but it does matter to those children who see a Black man as president. For those born in the past four or five years, having a Black president is not unusual. It's the norm. We can't ignore that reality either.

Marc: That's true. And that speaks to the complexity of being a Black person trying to make sense of a Black presidency. Like you, I had no illusions—I had been critical of Obama's centrist politics throughout the whole election cycle. I understood that he wasn't radically different than anything we've had before in terms of his stance on the economy, foreign policy or education. At the same time, I spent most of my time defending him on Fox News, because I felt he was the recipient of unfair criticism. In many ways, that's how I still feel. I'm deeply critical of the president, but I still feel enormous pride. I also feel very protective of him.

Mumia: So do I. That's why I was so secretly worried about his safety during the election. Like a lot of Black people, I didn't want to say what I feared, which was, *If he gets elected, they'll kill him.* It was a very real fear that millions of people felt but wouldn't express. It was almost like we were afraid to create a kind of collective jinx.

I remember talking to you and joking that when Obama wins, the first person he ought to thank in his acceptance speech is George W. Bush because without that idiot, none of this could be possible. And that's a fact. If it had been any other president than George, he never would've had a shot.

Marc: Wow! Why do you say that?

Mumia: I think George was just so poor. I mean, as a writer, reporter and an observer of the present American situation, I watched nearly all of George's press conferences. Hearing him talk was almost like the sound of fingernails across a chalkboard. My God, they were painful! And, of course, it didn't help that he was lying. "*Weapons of mass destruction!*"

Marc: Right! Right!

Mumia: For millions of White people he was an embarrassment. He showed them the worst possible example of a president. He made this young, attractive, well-educated, intelligent, well-spoken Black man look better and better. We forget that while Black and Hispanic folks' votes certainly helped, the majority of people who voted for Obama were White.

Marc: I agree to a certain extent. Obama definitely represented something different, and he emerged at the perfect moment: There was this bad presidency, as well as a war that young people were globally protesting. But there was something else about this particular moment. The Iraq war, combined with the lies about weapons of mass destruction, turned the public against the Bush administration's policies in a very public way, in a way I hadn't seen in my lifetime. I was at the anti-war rallies in the middle of the 2005 and 2006, and I had never seen moments like that when people were united so definitively around a single issue. So Obama came at the right moment. But even still, man…he's still a Negro, you know what I mean? In a world that doesn't love Negroes. It seems to me that it was more than the moment and more than George W. Bush's failures. It seemed to me that there was just no way that Obama could move into that space without there being a strong body of people who wanted him there. And I ain't talking about Black folks, White folks, or even voters. I'm talking about *real* decision-makers who had to have complete confidence that he could manage the American empire the same way the 43 White men before him did.

Mumia: That's exactly correct. There's a guy, Andrew Sullivan. He's a White, gay conservative Republican He was fully in support of the wars in Iraq and Afghanistan. But in the fall of 2007 he wrote an article in *The Atlantic* magazine that essentially argued why we need Obama. He talked about Obama's brown face, his Muslim heritage, and his father being from Kenya. He also talked about Obama's White background and how for the world, especially the Islamic world, his election would be a powerful propaganda coup. He argued that it would disable Al Qaeda and other jihadist movements to see a young man with that kind of background become the president of the United States because it would force them to say, "Wow this *is* an extraordinary country." And if you think about it, the people who celebrated Obama's victory the most, more than even Black Americans, were those on the African continent. Around the world people exclaimed what a great country this was. So there was a truth to what Sullivan argued.

Marc: Yes, because his narrative is exotic in a way that is extremely seductive. It's still stunning to think that the son of a Kenyan immigrant is the president of the most powerful empire in the history of the world. At the same time, his narrative is so exotic, so different than any other Black person's, that it renders him exceptional to the White body politic. It allows them to believe in America without having to re-imagine the humanity of Black people they know and come in regular contact with.

Mumia: It makes him exceptional, but it also makes him *acceptable*. Because he's not an American Negro in the sense that you and I claim. While his African family has a colonial background, they don't have a slavery background.

Marc: If President Obama had been of African-American descent, I think he would've experienced a different electoral outcome. In a very real way, being the descendants of slaves does shape one's worldview, political vision and aspirations. And it also shapes how the world sees the person. Obama's White mom and exotic Kenyan father becomes a story White people can love because it's a variation on the Horatio Alger narrative; it's a bootstrap narrative.

Mumia: It's Horatio Alger, but it's also the immigrant story. Remember, Obama played on that real strong: "*My father came here in the '60s,*" and so on. That rang in a lot of people's heads because, paradoxically, nothing is more central to the American self-image than the immigrant myth. That's the Genesis script for Americans, and only two groups of folks here really don't relate: so-called Indians and Black folks, because it was Indian country that got invaded and Black folks never asked to come here. But, *his* old man, Obama's old man, got on a plane willingly to come here! That ain't our overall story!

Marc: It's an interesting paradox. The president appeals to a quintessentially American immigrant narrative that says, "I am as American as you are." Yet, ironically so much of the attack on him from the Right has been animated by, "He's not from here. He is not one of us. He's not *ours*. He's Kenyan…" This is why the president continues to be dogged by the birther movement, which argues, quite literally, that President Obama isn't an American-born citizen. He's shown his full birth certificate and gotten sworn affidavits from every credible source imaginable, but a large sector of the country is still committed to the idea that Obama isn't from here. So it's an interesting double-edged sword we see him negotiating.

Mumia: There's an interesting dialectic that comes with foreignness, though. Malcolm X used to joke that there were certain restaurants he couldn't go to, but if he put a turban on his head they would treat him like a prince. Looking foreign gave him a kind of liberated living he couldn't experience as the descendent of a people who had been here for literally 500 years if you date our arrival from when Columbus brought Africans to Hispaniola.

Marc: Angela Davis said something similar in her autobiography. She talked about how she and her sister went into a shoe store in Alabama where they'd been treated poorly using fake French accents. With these accents, the same store that had given them second-class status suddenly saw them as special and different, allowing them to get first-class treatment. At the same time though, when you think of police violence victims like Abner Louima and Amadou Diallo and when you think of all the African folk who come here and still catch hell, who can't access jobs and health care, and who are just read as niggas on the street, there's a way in which we all become part of the same mix. And if they are read as being outside that mix, they become vulnerable to ethnic, religious and national profiling.

Mumia: That's absolutely true.

Marc: And keeping track of those two things is difficult, not just for White folk, but for Black folk. We accept Obama as ours because there's an advantage to it, both personally and politically. Still, I'm not sure we know what to do with him.

Mumia: We can claim Obama, but that don't make us his. You can claim him, but it ain't like he claiming you.

Marc: And that's what's frustrating to me. He ain't coming toward us. If anything, he's running from us.

Mumia: Under the first African-American president in the history of the most powerful empire ever, before Rome, look how Black folks who are poor and working are being treated. Also, look at little baby Aiyana Stanley-Jones, the 7-year-old who was shot by Detroit police in a reckless raid of her home. Look at Sean Bell, who New York City police shot to death the night before his wedding. The list goes on. Yet, Obama and his Justice Department have failed to address these issues in any significant way. No hate crime charges. No real stance against police brutality. And it's not just about the literal murders. It's also about the slow death that people experience when they lose their homes and can't get quality jobs, healthcare or education.

Marc: For sure. I didn't expect much else from him, so I can't say that I'm disappointed. But I'm still deeply saddened by the president's choices. I'm also saddened by the response of many Black people. Some of us still believe that Obama's approach is part of some kind of Machiavellian politics, where he's helping us from the side but not acknowledging us in public. Unfortunately, there's no evidence of that.

Mumia: If you didn't know dude was Black, nothing that he says or does would tell you. He doesn't talk about how Black folks are living in hell, economically, health-wise and educationally. He doesn't mention the prison industrial complex. Dude can't really talk about it. When he does mention it, he's the voice of the Right for the most part.

Marc: It's also crazy because at the same time that the Black president isn't addressing all of these issues plaguing Black America, there's also another movement emerging in direct response to him. According to recent polls, more Americans think there's more racism now than ever before. There's a Tea Party movement growing, there's a rise in White nationalist organizations. There was the Shirley Sherrod fiasco where a Civil Rights veteran was fired without discussion, investigation or benefit of the doubt, because Andrew Breitbart, a well-known, openly racist liar, targeted her. How does that play into the existence of a Black president? What does it all mean?

Mumia: Imagine all those Americans who woke up one morning and saw a Black man with a strange name on television. Then all of a sudden they hear that he wasn't born in the U.S. and he's a secret Kenyan Muslim terrorist. Despite all that hysteria, fueled by Glenn Beck, Dinesh D'Souza and others, no one talks about John McCain being born in Panama. And no one mentions that case law has established that if you're born anywhere on the planet, and your parent is American, you're American. They reacted with the same uninformed fear that they did when it was China and the so-called Yellow Peril, or in the '30s and '40s and '50s when it was the so-called Red Peril. It's the politics of fear, and it's very powerful because it works from the emotions. And the people whose emotions are pulled upon the most are those ethnic groups, like Italians and Jews, that weren't considered White until relatively recently. Given the way they're being recruited by conservatives, it's likely that Hispanics may be doing the same thing soon. That's why I refer to them as "probationary Whites." This is because power is seductive. There are Black people who bought into that. There are *Black* White supremacists who, because of their class have turned their backs on millions of poor and working class Black people. Why wouldn't light-skinned Hispanics kind of make that same bargain? Of course, some will, some won't.

Marc: But then there's this broader framework, where it doesn't matter how you self-identify because the world still imagines *you* in terms of race. So the idea that somehow White supremacy can sustain itself by shifting the terms of engagement and inclusion is fascinating; it's the idea that 30 years from now, who we consider White can encompass somebody like Bill Richardson, whom we currently consider Latino and celebrate for being a Clinton Administration minority appointee. Fifty years from now, he could be viewed no differently than an Italian, as a Sicilian who also might have some "ethnic" features but more or less lies under the rubric of Whiteness. That's terrifying business when you think about the architecture of White supremacy, and how malleable it is.

Mumia: This is not new. Whiteness has always been seen as a kind of property. Everybody wants to have it because it entitles you to everything the country has to offer. What's interesting now, however, is that there's also a certain kind of color consciousness that exists in this Obama age. One of the big reasons for this is hip-hop culture. Millions of young White kids grew up listening to hip-hop and saying, "Damn, that's cool!" They're so connected to aspects of Black culture that it was easier for them to vote for a Black president.

Marc: Oh, absolutely. Because now all of a sudden Whites have immediate and direct access to a certain kind of Black experience. They can play video games like "NBA Street," which allows users to play basketball in famous Black venues like Rucker Park in Harlem. They can watch television shows like "Pimp My Ride" or "Yo Momma" on MTV, which allow them to voyeuristically engage particular rituals of Black culture. Of course, these technologies weren't produced because of President Obama. He simply reflects and informs a set of conditions that are central to how many of us imagine race in the current moment. For Whites, Blackness has become a thing that can be tried on and engaged.

Whiteness is a property we all want to own because it entitles you to EVERYTHING.

Mumia: Tried on and modified.

Marc: Tried on, modified and commodified!

Mumia: Absolutely. And this helped Obama tremendously.

Marc: Yes, Obama was certainly the beneficiary of this modified and commodified Blackness. These processes, combined with his own racial idiosyncrasies, made him palatable and even human in the eyes of the White body politic. Even those who didn't vote for him had an easier time seeing him as a *person*. I'm just not sure that the rest of us have benefited in the same way. Many of those same White people who have the new Kanye West or 50 Cent album will still make decisions in the boardroom or the voting booth that operate against Black people's interest. So, at that level, their investment in Blackness becomes superficial and quite problematic.

Mumia: That again is a part of the flexibility of race. And it'll always be a danger to people of color. Black folks didn't choose who was Black. White power systems determined who wasn't White; you know, the old "one-drop" rule. There are Black folks in our community who would be White in Brazil, Cuba or Haiti, yet they all are Black here: physically, psychologically, socially and spiritually.

Marc: True. And the State institutionalizes these racial divisions and actually makes you make a choice. For example, on the U.S. Census form we've had to check "White," "Negro" or whatever. Other than checking "some other race," there's not a lot of space for the kind of racial complexity or hybridism that actually exists in 21st century America. The president himself checks "Black" for a lot of political and personal reasons, but he's an amalgamation of a whole bunch of stuff. And on the Census, including the 2010 one that came out in the midst of Obama's first term, you have to make these choices that demographically encourage or even demand that certain folk choose White or "Other."

Mumia: Well, we cannot forget the fundamental fact that this is a White supremacist society. And in fact we're founded upon that basis. One of the first acts of Congress, in 1790, was a federal law that essentially said that only White people could become naturalized citizens of the United States. And that stood for well over a century. There are great cases from the 1800s to the early 1900s of people trying to—to put it crudely—join the White club. I mean, you had Syrians, right?

Marc: Right!

Mumia: They were filing suit in federal court saying, "Look I'm a Syrian" or "I'm a Palestinian" or something like that. They were like, *"Jesus came from my clan or my nation. So, you trying to say Jesus ain't White?"*

Marc: You'd think that'd put them against the wall!

Mumia: But of course they were like, *"You may be Caucasian, but that ain't the same as White. We don't care about Jesus. We know what White is, and we know you ain't!"* That kind of thing. And then you had Japanese-Americans who were born here, and when they'd go visit Japan they wouldn't be allowed to return. They'd be told, "Your passport isn't good." All of these groups fought desperately to be declared White and most of them failed because, of course, you had White judges who were like, *"We can't define it through scientific certainty, but we know what White is and what it ain't. You ain't White."*

Marc: Right! *"We know it when we see it."*

Mumia: *"We know it when we smell it. And you smell funny!"*

Marc: We still see those same fights to protect or to close ranks around Whiteness in ways that often even marginalize disenfranchised people who have deep cultural commitments or historical ties to a particular nation-state. And it's happening all around the globe. You have right now, for example, Algerians in France. I'm not talking about people who just got there. I'm talking about three generations of Algerians in France who, no matter how much they buy into French culture, how well they speak the language, how invested they are in the political aspirations of France, they are still not considered French. And France makes no bones about telling them that.

Mumia: It's not just France. Look at Germany, where you have Turks who've lived there for three or four generations. Many know no Turkish and their only home has been Germany. But by law, to this day, you have to have German blood to be considered German; meaning you have German ancestors. Living there or being born there isn't enough. That's happening here in the United States, too. Think about this: There is currently a fight over the 14th Amendment, about whether people born here are actually citizens. They're painting it as a fight against the illegal immigration of Mexicans, but who's next?

Marc: The most amazing thing is how we can buy into this logic. Yes, there are political and economic benefits to accepting particular racial identities, but it's still mind-boggling the way people actually believe these notions against all common-sense evidence to the contrary. For example, you can go to Sudan and see Arabs in the North who are fighting Sudanese in the North. A lot of those Northern Arabs, in places like Khartoum or Omdurman, are brown! When you look at Saudi Arabians, they're brown, too!

Mumia: And some are straight-up Black! Again, race is a fairly recent human construct. And while I'm not one of those people who say race is a completely false construct—there's truth and reality to it—race is a very recent thing, very flexible thing. And for millions of people in this country who are identified on their Census forms, or on their passports as White, if they were to go to Britain they would be declared Black and non-white. If you're Pakistani, for example, you wouldn't be considered White in Britain. The Brits have a very clear idea of what Whiteness is. You might be light-skinned, your skin might be lighter than mine, or mine is redder than yours, but guess what? You ain't White.

Marc: Right.

Mumia: And they accept that. And when you hear people talk about Black people in the British context, they could be talking about Pakistanis, Asians, Japanese you name it. Because their binary is Black and White.

Racial logic is CONVOLUTED in the age of Obama.

Marc: But on some level that binary is really just White and Other, because White is normalized and everything else is measured against it. In Italy recently there has been a public conversation about the so-called gypsies, the Romanis. Italian authorities pretty much announced that, in a short period of time, they are going to be completely gone. Because of their dark skin, the Italian government talks about Romanis as these foreign, alien Others. This is particularly ironic given the fact that Italians themselves are marked in racially complex and often ambiguous terms. Think about all the brothers who get called out for interracial dating and defend themselves by saying "She ain't White, she's Italian!"

Mumia: That's definitely the old-school excuse!

Marc: Yeah, but nine times out of 10, she's not saying to her parents, "It's Okay. It's not like we're White. We're Italian!" And if she is, it ain't workin'! I say all of that to say that it's fascinating to see how dynamic and convoluted racial logic is in the age of Obama. Obviously, this doesn't begin with Obama, but some of us would like to think that these differences are getting elided, or that the contours are getting flattened out. But things are getting messier and messier.

Mumia: No doubt.

Marc: One of the most fascinating polls that I've encountered is one that shows that more White Americans believe Obama is Muslim today, as we're having this conversation, than two years ago when he was first elected president. Given all the available evidence out here to the contrary, "Obama is a Muslim," has to be a proxy for something else. The number of White folks who believe it reflects a very real anxiety. It's just like when Black approval ratings are really high for the president. We'll approve of Obama at a 90 percent rate when the rest of the nation is at 30 or 40 percent. It's not that we don't know that sometimes he's messin' up or don't have serious critiques of his job performance. But our approval is a vote against White supremacy. It's a vote of protection for somebody who we feel is being unfairly assailed. Similarly, I have to assume that all these White folk don't think that Obama is secretly making salat on the East Wing of the White House. But "Muslim" becomes a proxy for something else. Islam becomes a pejorative that's used to mark his supposed otherness. It's used to mark the foreignness of a president who—and this is the ironic thing for me—above everything has imposed and sustained a set of rules and policies that only reinforce the power of the very people doing the marking! It's not like he's radically changed the way multinational corporations function. Obama bailed out corporate America in record proportion. He hasn't enhanced the welfare state. In many ways, he's pushed forward a political agenda that's less progressive than Bill Clinton's. He's as mainstream as they come. So race comes to trump reason when it comes to mainstream politics and public discourse.

Mumia: Absolutely. I mean, from my political perspective, I can express a kind of disappointment in his political stances. But it is a fact that the Troubled Asset Relief Program bailout saved this economy from a level of disaster that most of us, no matter where we are on the spectrum, don't want to contemplate. He saved this economy from almost certain destruction. How he did that is, of course, questionable. But the fact that it was done is not even up for debate.

OBAMA is completely supporting the national agenda when it comes to war and other matters, but he still doesn't get right wing support.

Marc: Right. And he did it with the logic of free-market capitalism. It wasn't like he did some radical thing. He did just what any American president would do.

Mumia: That's right. And not just that, if you look at his foreign policy, he's profoundly nationalistic. That is, American nationalist, not Black nationalist. He dropped more bombs in six months than George Bush did in three years. There are also the Special Forces in Pakistan doing their thing. We ain't even talking about the drones.

Marc: Right, my God! Predator drones are everywhere destroying innocent human life. And that's what's so stunning about all this. He's in this ignoble paradox where he's being as nationalistic and imperialistic as he can be yet he'll never receive full support from a mainstream body politic that treats him as a subversive foreigner. He's doing the best possible rendition of a White president, and can't even get credit for it.

Mumia: Because race trumps everything.

Marc: Word.

FOR YOUR LIBRARY

From Savage to Negro, **Lee D. Baker**

Globalization and Race, **Kamari Maxine Clarke and Deborah A. Thomas, eds.**

The Substance of Hope, **William Jelani Cobb**

Critical Race Theory, **Kimberle Crenshaw, et al**

The Souls of Black Folk, **W.E.B. Du Bois**

Presidential Race, **Michael Eric Dyson**

Politics After Hope, **Henry A. Giroux**

How The Irish Became White, **Noel Ignatiev**

Racial Paranoia, **John L. Jackson**

Racial Formation, **Michael Omi and Howard Winant**

More Beautiful and More Terrible, **Imani Perry**

"Goodbye to All That: Why Obama Matters," **Andrew Sullivan,** in *The Atlantic* **(Dec. 2007)**

The Price of Racial Reconciliation, **Ronald W. Walters**

Alchemy of Race and Rights, **Patricia J. Williams**

Between Barack and a Hard Place, **Tim Wise**

CHAPTER 3

Bigger Than Hip-Hop: Black Cultural Politics

From our very first meeting, we quickly bonded over our common love of Black culture. In fact, it has been impossible for us to talk about any subject without incorporating everything from visual art to film, music to architecture. But our investment in culture isn't merely personal. We recognize the role culture plays in shaping and reflecting the experiences of Black people in America. In this conversation, we explore this role and arrive at new levels of understanding about the power and limits of culture as a form of expression and political resistance.

Marc: Culture is inescapable. Even politics and the economy can be understood as cultural systems. For Black folk, culture has been a primary window into our experience here in America.

Mumia: I agree. And today, the biggest phenomenon in Black culture, not to mention global culture, is hip-hop. Hip-hop is far closer to your generation than it is to mine. You also wrote a book, *Beats, Rhymes, and Classroom Life*, so you've studied this thing and obviously thought about it in depth. What are your ideas on it?

Marc: I struggle with hip-hop, man. In some ways, I see it as a revolutionary *form*, in the sense that it shows what Black folk can do. When you think about poor Black kids in post-industrial Bronx, New York, taking grandma's records in the basement and turning them into a global art form. When you think about afterschool programs being shut down and young people having no access to musical instruments, so they turn the turntable into an instrument. I mean, it's really a testimony to Black genius and, in that sense, it's revolutionary. At the same time, it pays tribute to the best aspects of our culture, from America to the Caribbean to the continent of Africa. But I also struggle with hip-hop since, I think, at this moment in history it's become a revolutionary *form* that's devoid of revolutionary *content*. And there are a lot of ways to think about that. I mean, on the most basic level, it's troublesome because of the literal content. You turn on the radio and you hear all the misogyny, violence, homophobia and consumerism. But in some sense, I think that's a superficial or at least insufficient critique. We can all point to trifling lyrics not just in hip-hop but in any genre. What troubles me about hip-hop right now, though, is the deeper issue of political economy; the record labels that co-opt it. At least in mainstream American hip-hop, the culture gets co-opted. I mean, think about our brothers M-1 and stic-man from dead prez. Their first album was one of the most beautiful and revolutionary albums that I've ever heard. But it's put out through Sony. So even if I spend $10 to support Mutulu and stic, about $9 of that $10 is going to Sony Music Entertainment so they can promote someone else who is performing and promoting the counter-revolutionary identity of the drug dealer or the pimp. So I struggle with it. And not just on an abstract or political level. As a father, I hate the fact that I have to censor so much of the music that defines my daughter's generation. At the same time, I cannot let her consume music that undermines her very sense of humanity.

Mumia: I would dispute your description of hip-hop as "revolutionary," coming from the kind of hardcore revolutionary political formation of my youth. We weren't using "revolution" as a metaphor, but as a thing that was not only real but imminent. But I think you sustained it, arguing

I dispute the description of hip-hop as "revolutionary." Coming up, we didn't use REVOLUTION as a metaphor, but as a thing that was very real.

"revolutionary" in the American sense of the term. Revolutionary in American lingo means "that which is new." They took something that was old, discarded, considered garbage, and created something incredibly new. They produced a whole new sound that literally took the world, and continues to take the world, by storm. People all around the world are bumping their heads to hip-hop beats. They may not rap in English.

They may rap in their mother tongues. But they're informed and encapsulated and motivated and, in many instances, inspired by hip-hop. And the Black freedom struggle, you see.

So I share your concern, obviously. Because the revolutionary form without the revolutionary content is disturbing. It's kind of like a mask you wear on Halloween; not a mask in the frightening sense, but in the sense that it's not your real face, and it's certainly not your real heart, fears and dreams.

Marc: Right.

Mumia: There are some artists, of course, who are doing that. But from my vantage point, I can't say most are doing it. Those who are doing it are quite extraordinary. And I don't mean those who say things on their records but those who are speaking *off* the records about their lives in America. They are extremely rare and when you do hear them, many seem to be profoundly uninformed. This morning, when I was thinking about calling you, I was thinking about Kanye West after Katrina. He got up in front of the telethon cameras and said, "George Bush don't care about Black people." It was like a thunderclap.

Marc: Why do you think it resonated so much with people?

Mumia: Because it was a profound, simple, powerful truth. And I'll never forget Mike Myers, Kanye's co-host, looking into the camera like a deer in headlights. I didn't know if that was Mike Myers or Dr. Evil! But it was like, *"Oh shit! What have we here?"*

Marc: And I think that's the power of it. In the Black Power era, we had a Black Arts movement that supported our Civil Rights struggle. But I think the difference was that the artists were allies to and workers within a struggle that had political organization and hardcore, committed leadership. In the 1960s and 1970s, they talked about the Civil Rights and Black Power movements. They were defined by their politics. Now, they call us the hip-hop generation. We're being defined by the culture. Our culture is an outgrowth of our politics but in some ways it seems like we're expecting this cultural form to *be* the politics.

Mumia: That's a good analysis. I was reading a collection of essays by Amiri Baraka a few months ago. In them, he was really inspired by hip-hop because, of course, these are young poets first and foremost.

Marc: Well, some are. I think there are a lot of folk out there who see rapping as a pathway to money and fame. And you can tell from the lyrics. Many have compromised any sense of artistic integrity for mainstream appeal.

Mumia: Absolutely. And those folk are becoming the majority, at least in the mainstream. But still, there's a group that's keeping the tradition alive. So there is continuity, in a sense, from the Black Arts movement to a new generation using words with vision and beats behind them to create wordscapes of their lives, their reality, their fears. So Baraka's loving it while attacking the corporate element that you mentioned earlier, how the distributors tried to control the cultural creators.

Marc: Exactly! And that was the turn in the late 1980s, early 1990s. We had that high moment with Sister Souljah and Paris and Public Enemy, which turned into N.W.A and Snoop Dogg real fast. And to some extent, people see that moment as the decline of hip-hop culture, and the end of the romantic era of cultural nationalism personified by folks like the Native Tongues, Brand Nubian and Arrested Development. That said, I felt that the cultural nationalist movement was less interesting and less politically powerful than the West Coast gangster rap that followed it.

Mumia: Why do you say that?

Marc: Because gangster rap represented the cohort that Huey P. Newton often idealized: the lumpenproletariat—the pimps, the pushers and the thugs, the ones who had been rejected and despised by society. These were the people Tupac was talking about during his last years. In that regard, gangster rap marked hip-hop's best opportunity to produce something that was truly revolutionary. Not just revolutionary in the sense that I articulated and you wisely critiqued earlier, but in a substantive way. But we were unable to sustain the movement because we became prisoner to our own vices, our own glorification of the very things that we were trying to critique. Violence, drugs, sex and materialism were not only central themes of the music, they were explicitly and implicitly glorified without an adequate countervailing critique. Revolution of any sort must be a humanistic and morally defensible project. Sadly, we never sufficiently engaged in the kind of self-critique and collective development necessary for revolutionary art, much less revolutionary struggle.

Mumia: During the '60s, we were awash in revolutionary art, much of which didn't survive into the '80s and '90s. Folks were productive at a high level, driven by the movement itself. There were plays and films from groups like Liberation Newsreel. People assembled in church basements to see Arthur Hall's African dance troupe. Groups like the Black Panther Party met at the Church of the Advocate in North Philly. In storefronts, people

Gangster rap represented the cohort that Huey P. Newton often IDEALIZED: the pimps, the pushers and the gangsters.

were bursting with passion and purpose. And music?! Music, especially in the funk era, was an atomic bomb of cultural consciousness. Think of War, Sly and the Family Stone, Earth Wind and Fire, Con Funk Shun—whoa! James Brown's "Say it Loud: I'm Black and I'm Proud!" There were periods of revolutionary flowering, driven by the movement itself. But much of the material from that era—in anthropological terms, the artifacts of that culture—did not survive into the succeeding eras and did not properly water the grasslands, shrubs, trees and rivers to come. And then, along came rap. That changed the game.

Marc: No doubt. And the residue of revolutionary love from that moment is what I see lacking in so much of the stuff we're doing today. Where's the art that is not only aesthetically avant-garde, but also challenges us to love ourselves in newer and deeper ways? Think about how important gospel music was to our ancestors. It allowed them to love and believe in themselves despite all the adversity of the world. I also know how profoundly I was affected by Assata's poetry or Common's lyrics

Where is the art that's not only avant-garde but also challenges us to LOVE ourselves in newer and deeper ways?

on *Like Water For Chocolate* and *Be*. Sadly, the culture industry turns a blind eye to this love deficit as long as it is adversely affecting Black people. For example, think about when Ice-T came out with the controversial "Cop Killer" song. The nation was up in arms because they worried about the consequences of making music that encouraged violence against law enforcement. While I don't dispute that sentiment, what about the rest of the gangster rap movement? How many songs were made about "killing niggas" and nobody said a thing? Why is our threshold for Black misery so high?

Mumia: Exactly. Exactly. So, what is rewarded and what is repressed? When you look at the long, wide, deep scope of Black culture, or performance culture more broadly, what is at the core? The urge for freedom, right?

Marc: Absolutely. As oppressed people, our thirst for freedom is apparent throughout all of our culture.

Mumia: When you listen to John Coltrane do "A Love Supreme" it's about freedom. The freedom to be human. To be courageous in a country that says, "You're not human, you have no creativity, and even if you have it, we're gonna steal it." So I think that, at its core, that urge for freedom was certainly present at the birth of hip-hop. And you hear less of that now because of the market forces that have controlled, distributed and ultimately edited out some of the hardcore stuff there at the beginning.

Marc: I agree. That's why I'm most inspired when I hear hip-hop that is outside the reach of multinational corporations. For example, I was in Tanzania, the summer before last. I wasn't even in a major city like Dar es Salaam; I was in a small village in the Northern part of Arusha. Brothers and sisters had tires on their feet for shoes, but they knew Tupac, man! They knew Jay-Z. These guys have a global impact. But what was most noteworthy and inspirational wasn't that they could recognize global hip-hop symbols. It was that they'd begun to craft their own kind of narrative, their own kind of hip-hop that speaks to their specific issues, conditions and concerns. And over time, those narratives became baptized within their own cultural traditions. Take Cuba, for example. When you listen to Cuban hip-hop groups like Primera Base or the Orishas, their early albums sounded like 1990s American hip-hop, just in Spanish. But you fast-forward 10 years, man, and they got salsa, bachata and merengue rhythms mixed in. They have a kind of Cuban revolutionary political edge to the songs that make it their own thing. And ain't nobody buying and selling that on a global marketplace the way they are Tupac or Jay-Z.

Mumia: Well sure. I think the inherent power in the revolutionary art form is that it's taken by other communities and becomes even more revolutionary, right?

Marc: And that's why I keep holding on to the idea that hip-hop is a revolutionary *form*. I just don't have a lot of hope that we can do much with it here in the United States in the service of political struggles of the 21st century. How central was art and culture for the struggles of the '60s and '70s?

Mumia: Well, to be perfectly honest, it wasn't. When I was in the Black Panther Party, we were involved in, frankly, a life and death struggle with people we called "cultural nationalists." And we went so hard against them; many of us considered them enemies, as opposed to contemporaries and even colleagues with a different political perspective. The older I get and the further I get away in time from that era, I realize the mistake of that period. Not just within the Party, but of Party leadership.

Marc: What was your beef with the cultural nationalists?

Mumia: Well, I think it took on ideological tones. Huey used to say, "Cultural nationalists talk about it, but they ain't really about it," and, "They don't really rumble," and "Writing a poem is not going to get the oppressor off our back." Those sorts of things. Of course, there's a certain truth to that. But it's also true that poetry is a form of resistance. I was just reading Howard Zinn, and he said something that wowed me because I was thinking about you and me. In one of his last books, *A Power Governments Cannot Suppress*, he said, "Rebellion often starts as something cultural." And as I thought about those old struggles, and I look at the struggles that young Black America is going through today, I know that much of what they're suffering from is really a result of a cultural war against them. Hip-hop began as something that could be called profoundly oppositional to the governing narrative about the world and about Black youth.

Marc: Absolutely. And even though a lot of early hip-hop focused on partying and having fun, it still challenged the governing narrative of young people as civic terrors.

Mumia: That's exactly right. And the more political stuff served as a direct challenge to White supremacy, capitalism, unbridled materialism, all those kinds of things. The songs had an oppositional tone and feel. *"Don't mess with me! Get off my back!"* was the theme, but that changed. If I were a broker on Wall Street—a crazy idea I know—I could appropriate a lot of what's in hip-hop and, if I were in my Benz or my Bentley, I could turn on a lot of hip-hop and love it because it's talking about money!

Marc: Yes!

Mumia: And the institution of money.

Marc: Exactly. It's become a quintessentially American, hyper-capitalist narrative, for sure.

Mumia: Ain't no opposition! By promoting wealth acquisition as the end-all be-all, they ignore a simple fact: No matter how much money and cultural capital you acquire, you still a nigga in America.

Marc: Let's backtrack for a minute. I'm still fascinated by these internecine battles of the '60s and the notion of concrete politics versus cultural politics. I feel like nowadays, my folk, particularly intellectuals of my generation, have moved to the other extreme. Now, it feels as if cultural politics becomes the primary way that we talk about resistance and activism. So we'll talk about the resistance of a rap song, such as N.W.A saying, "Fuck the police!" but there's no organized movement behind it anymore. We merely celebrate the symbolic. Or, when we look back at our history, we'll talk about slaves who spat in the greens or workers who slowed down on the assembly line as an everyday form of resistance. The work of brilliant scholars like James Scott and Robin D.G. Kelley provide powerful examples of this phenomenon. And I'm cool with that type of analysis, as there's much to be said about micro-level acts of resistance, not to mention fashion and music and sights and spectacles as a form of politics and expression. My only worry is that we've come to overstate the value of these practices and wind up doing the very thing that ya'll were scared of in the '60s. I worry that we don't have an authentic, concrete politics anymore. I'm not quite sure how to balance, or even think about those two things.

Mumia: Here's the key to what you just said: "no organized movement." There it is. During the '60s and '70s, The Movement was ubiquitous. It was North, South, East, West. It was the States, the U.K., the Caribbean, Africa, Asia, know what I mean? And that movement fed the music, the arts, film, theatre, etcetera. Do you remember that old black and white flick, *The Organization*? It featured Sidney Poitier, I believe. He played a real militant cat and was part of a radical formation in a Northern city. It reflected how art imitates life; life ain't really supposed to imitate art. But, what distinguished the era from what came before and after it, was the absence of fear. We thought the Revolution was right around the corner; that it was so close you could touch it!

Marc: I'm glad you said that, as it leads into another question I have about how you understood Black cultural life within a post-revolutionary context. If the revolution was right around the corner, what did you think would happen if you'd won? What would Black culture look like after the revolution?

Mumia: Well, of course we took a lot of our ideological and thinking points from Huey P. Newton. He said that if we look at Africa, and use that as a kind of template for African-American cultural development, we'd find very few places that have not been contaminated by imperialism and colonialism. We're looking at something that is profoundly unnatural, he argued. And he also echoed a point made by Frantz Fanon, who was really important for Huey's growth and for the development of the Party. Fanon was very critical of bourgeois nationalism and cultural nationalism. He spoke about how the African bourgeoisie will change the name of a country and "Africanize" a lot of things that change it back from its colonial parents. But what they won't change is their relationship to the European power and the European economy that exploited the labor and the resources of the African nation. And how true is that?

Marc: That's real. This is why it's so important to think about culture as more than just rituals and practices and holidays, or even as proxies for race and ethnicity. We must also think about the economy, the political economy, as a cultural system with its own cultural logic. Otherwise we end up exhausting all of our intellectual and spiritual energy reimagining the more superficial or at least visible dimensions of culture without acknowledging the ways that late capitalism and White supremacy, to name just a few things, remain normalized within our collective imaginations. That's how you can end up with African nation-states that are post-colonial politically, but deeply committed to European aesthetics, religious practices and worldviews. Or, as Fanon and Huey are describing, an African nation-state that has a post- or pre-colonial cultural veneer, but sustains a colonial relationship to capital.

Mumia: Exactly! I mean, think of Mobutu. He changed his name from Sergeant Joseph Desire Mobutu to Mobutu Sese Seko. He wore a leopard skin cap. He walked around with a cane. He changed the name of the Congo to Zaire and he also changed the names of many cities within the country to traditional African names. But did he change the relationship of capital to the oppressed? No. And that's the fundamental relationship.

Marc: Even worse, he terrorized his people and drained the treasury!

Mumia: I hear you. But my point is that he did all of the cultural things—and Huey was reminding us of that even then, through the writings of Fanon. Unfortunately though, rather than really struggling with brothers and sisters who were in more culturally influenced organizations, we saw them as enemies. And of course, there were wars between us. There were deaths between us, bro. And once it got to that stage, we couldn't hear each other. We really couldn't see each other. And I think they lost something for their failed communication with us and we also lost something, something profound, in our failure to communicate with them.

What would Black CULTURE look like after the revolution?

Marc: So if you could re-imagine it, what would you do now? Would you incorporate cultural nationalism into the political struggles of the party? Would there be a space for that? Or would you simply not be as dismissive of them?

Mumia: We can't rewrite yesterday. But think about this—the powerful impact of one of the most hated figures of that period: Maulana Karenga. Karenga has impacted the lives of millions of people with Kwanzaa. And that's just one of his contributions. But he clearly has impacted the lives of millions of people. I found myself, as a young parent, incorporating Kwanzaa as a cultural expression. Otherwise, what kind of expression do Black kids get from TV? Or even from our music? None of that.

Marc: Right.

Mumia: So I had to swallow my pride and say, "Yeah, this is a good thing."

Marc: Kwanzaa is an interesting one because it's resisting the European Christmas tradition at the same time that it's honoring the African tradition of gift giving around the winter solstice, around the community collective, around family, and around humanistic principals. I feel that. I think what I struggle with, even now, are the brands of cultural nationalism that still reflect a bourgeois obsession with European values. I mean, for example, look at the neo-soul movement, which people generally see as a positive. And, on an aesthetic level, I agree. When artists like Erykah Badu, Jill Scott and D'Angelo hit the scene in the late '90s, it was refreshing to see the beauty of locs and sarongs and braids spotlighted on a national and international stage. But, unlike the Black Arts movement, this was a very middle class project that was often completely disconnected from any kind of political resistance. Where's the political dimension of neo-soul? And I understand that we ain't got to be politically engaged at literally every moment. After all, there must also be space for pleasure, playfulness, escape, desire and even eroticism within everyday life. But I think there should be a broader politics that informs the art, even in subtle ways, at every moment. I haven't always seen that.

Mumia: Your point is very well taken. After all, it's cultural nationalism that inspired a lot of the bourgeoisie in Black America. You can wear your hair or clothes in a certain way, but unless you engage with the revolutionary transformation of the day-to-day lives of millions of our people—that is, create new ways of surviving, of resisting—then you just wear your hair a certain way. And capitalism will sell you the grease to put in your head!

Marc: Exactly! We sometimes fail to see how our symbolic acts of resistance get co-opted as well. So the same "dreadlocks" that might've been a sign of resistance, and even conjured fear within the colonial imagination, can be used on fashion runways and Benetton ads. Even Bob Marley! Songs like "One Love" no longer signify African diasporic unity, but rather an empty "colorblind" multiculturalism that has no political teeth.

You damned sure won't hear "Crazy Baldheads" or "Slave Driver" in an ad.

Mumia: But, we've gotta remember that this is a capitalist system that, well, "marketizes" everything. Why not co-opt Black culture? They've been doing that for over 100 years! Dig this: a few months ago, I read Rickey Vincent's book, *Funk*, where he cited something called the "Appropriation-Revitalization Syndrome," where White marketing interests appropriate Black art forms, water them down, and then mainstream them to the masses. They been doing this since brothers and sisters were working in the fields, in chains, singing spirituals to keep their spirits up during the rampant repression. So, from way back, authentic Black art forms have been co-opted, rendered safe for popular (read: White) consumption and then exploited.

Marc: I worry about where Black culture is headed as it becomes more and more integrated into broader American, and indeed, global culture. As our resistance continues to get co-opted, what does the next cultural moment look like? And how can we construct it in a way that actually leads to liberation, instead of replicating the same conditions?

Black art forms have been co-opted, rendered safe for popular consumption, and then exploited.

Mumia: The question must be, "Is this expression oppositional or is it acquiescent? Does it challenge what needs to be challenged or does it roll over and play dead?" Once that becomes the central frame, then the answer to your question becomes clear. Even in our church, which is perhaps now one of the most conservative institutions in the Black community—it began as something profoundly oppositional.

Marc: Right.

Mumia: That's why churches were bombed in the '60s. Because that's where Black folk got together, organized and began movements. Social transformation. You cannot say that there are sites of opposition today, despite the rash of church burnings across the South. Those were an expression of rampant White supremacy, but not of fear of our organizing.

We should never acquiesce to something that doesn't SERVE our larger and ongoing humanity, strength and spirit.

Marc: Right. But the other question for me is, "opposition to what?" Because some would say that in the Black church today, people are just surviving. Just being in the church, or any other place that offers a narrative that says you are a full human being, is also a kind of resistance, right. Even if there's no concrete politics attached to it.

Mumia: Absolutely. Especially in *this* context, because we live in a White supremacist, anti-human, capitalist context. Because there is a narrative and a discourse functioning in America that says, "Black ain't human." You dig?

Marc: Word.

Mumia: Anything about us that's humanistic is resistant. But we are either opposing something or we are acquiescent to something. And we should never acquiesce to something that doesn't serve our larger and ongoing humanity, strength and spirit. That's my point.

Marc: That's real, and that spirit of resistance has to live through the next phase of whatever our culture is. I don't know what it's gonna look like, but I know that resistance is the precondition for it, man.

Mumia: And I know it's gonna be oppositional because that's *our* reality in this culture

FOR YOUR LIBRARY

LeRoi Jones /Amiri Baraka Reader,
Amiri Baraka (William J. Harris, ed.)

Theatre of the Oppressed, Augusto Boal

Can't Stop, Won't Stop, Jeff Chang

To the Break of Dawn, William Jelani Cobb

Hip-Hop Japan, Ian Condry

Black Skin, White Masks, Frantz Fanon

Race Rebels and *Yo' Mama's Disfunktional!*, Robin D.G. Kelley

Visions of a Liberated Future, Larry Neal,
Amiri Baraka and Stanley Crouch

Soul Babies, Mark Anthony Neal

Class Notes, Adolph L. Reed

Domination and the Arts of Resistance and *Weapons of the Weak*, James C. Scott

Funk, Rickey Valmont

A Power Governments Cannot Suppress, Howard Zinn

CHAPTER 4

Black Leadership: A Continuing Crisis?

Given the range of problems confronting the Black community, there is little doubt that there's a demand for political, intellectual and moral leadership. Sadly, perhaps more than any other moment in history, there is a dangerous absence of such leadership within our most vital institutions. In this conversation, we critically examine current and previous approaches to Black leadership, locating valuable lessons from both our successes and our failures. Through this conversation, we aim to offer a sober but hopeful vision for principled, courageous and visionary Black leadership.

Mumia: In *Breaking Bread*, his book with bell hooks, Cornel West says, "There is a profound crisis in Black leadership… [N]o one who is willing to be prophetic, in a bold and defiant manner, with a deep all-inclusive moral vision, and a sophisticated analysis of the distribution of wealth, and power and resources in our society. Black politicians can't do it because they're locked in the mode of compromise. They cannot speak with boldness and defiance, and hence, most don't. On the other hand, the Civil Rights leaders themselves are not talking about class, gender, and empire. They don't want to give a critique of multinational corporations, probably because those corporations are helping undergird their own organizations."

Marc: What's important about this quote is that it's not only spot on, but that it was articulated 20 years ago. It's sad that very little has changed with regard to the quality of Black leadership.

Mumia: And if things have changed, they've changed for the worse. Especially when you look at the conditions in the Black community on the one hand, and the explosion of the prison industrial complex on the other. Both of those things speak to the absence of real Black leadership. Black leaders today are far more numerous, but they're far more cautious. They're far less tied to Black working class people and they're far less effective. The same can be said about the Civil Rights movement.

Marc: That's real. And that quote you just read from 20 years ago could've been written 50 years ago or it could've been written today, if we think about the intersections of race, class, gender and empire. This is especially true when we talk about the lack of a prophetic voice and, quite frankly, just a lack of courage on the Black leadership front. So many of today's

There's a lack of COURAGE among Black leaders.

leaders aren't trying to disrupt power, they just want to become power-brokers. There are a lot of us who are considered leaders often without real scrutiny of the term and all it requires. You and I are both considered leaders, but I'm always reluctant to accept that term because I'm not exactly sure what it even means at this moment. I teach at an Ivy League school. I've worked for major media outlets. So I'm certainly visible. And while I like to think I take courageous stands—shit, talking to you is a courageous stand on some level…

Mumia: Absolutely!

Marc: But at the end of the day I wonder, "*Do I satisfy the conditions or qualifications for being a leader?*" While I see you as an indisputable leader, I don't think I've arrived there yet. I see it as a work in progress. Unfortunately I think many of us, including me, are given that title too quickly, before we've earned it. And when I look into the broader sphere, at the Civil Rights leadership of today, at the activist organizations of today, I don't see the kind of vision, courage and moral character requisite for strong Black leadership. I'm curious about your thoughts, though. Has it ever really existed? Is there a leadership vacuum at this historical moment that's somehow greater or more profound than, say, in the 1950s or 1960s?

Mumia: I actually think that there was a time when there was stronger leadership. I mean, of course, we have a tendency to look back at the past as this golden era, when in fact there was no golden era. Still, there was a time when Black leaders were forced to grow—because of the burgeoning, expanding and, really, exploding Black movement—in order to remain relevant. When you read the writings of Martin Luther King, Jr., you can see his transition from this very cautious petit-bourgeois preacher to a voice for those who were not in his choir, who were not of his church. Think about Martin Luther King speaking out against the Vietnam War and the hell he caught from other Black leaders. They were like, *"Whoa! Talk about the inner city but don't be talking about no empire in Vietnam."* King's group lost money. His most intimate leader-colleagues turned against him. The White press, to a man, turned on him.

Marc: Right. Exactly! There are three things that you just said that resonated with me. One, even though you didn't say it explicitly, is that the leadership at that moment was so damn young, man! Martin Luther King dies at 39. Malcom X dies at 39. Che Guevara dies at 39. All were leading movements at a young age.

Many of our current leaders are people who knocked their fathers off the stage but WON'T let their sons or daughters on.

Mumia: That's right!

Marc: So leadership was incredibly young at that moment in history. At this moment in history it seems as if leadership is not as young. Or, better put, there is plenty of young leadership, but the dominant voices on the scene are the same voices we've had for 30 or 40 years. I've worked with some of these leaders and many of them are people who knocked their fathers off the stage but won't let their sons or daughters get on.

Mumia: Exactly. So the strong, young Black leaders around the country never get a chance to do what they're capable of doing. What we *need* them to do.

Marc: Right. And, of course, there are exceptions. Ben Jealous has injected some youthful energy into the NAACP, even if I disagree with some of his strategies. There are also radical voices like Fred Hampton, Jr.'s in Chicago. And across the country, there are many strong, young voices in the Malcolm X Grassroots Movement. But they don't get the attention that they should because there's such a focus on old school leaders. And that's frustrating because what made those movements so powerful was—

Mumia: —the youth!

Marc: I mean, Fred Hampton, Sr. is in Chicago organizing when he's—

Mumia: —20 years old! When Huey founded the Black Panther Party, he was 24. And like you said, the old heads don't want to get off the stage. But the real deal is, you can't ask permission. I mean, Huey didn't ask for permission. He didn't write to Andy Young and Martin King and say, "Can I be down? Do you guys really mind?"

Marc: Right! Right!

Mumia: You gotta take the stage. You gotta bum-rush the mic sometimes.

Marc: You took the words right out of my mouth. They bum-rushed the show, man. And that connects to the second thing that resonated with me, which is an ethic of risk. You know, they were committed to risking their very lives in the service of freedom. When we look at how many people were railroaded. When we look through COINTELPRO—forget everything else, forget all of our so-called speculation, just look at the stuff that even the government doesn't dispute—we see so many Black leaders being taken out. People who were set up for kidnapping and bank robbery, people who were accused of being terrorists. We've seen the whole gamut of things. And many brothers and sisters knew when going into the movements that this was going to happen. I can't tell you how many activists from the '60s tell me that they didn't pay their phone bill for three years...

Mumia: And the phone stayed on!

Marc: The government kept that phone on! So it's an ethic of risk that I see at the best moments of leadership. Not just in the 1960s, but even when we think about Du Bois, Marcus Garvey, Harriet Tubman or Ella Baker. There was always this ethic of risk that stands in sharp contrast to the current lack of political courage.

Mumia: When you talk about COINTELPRO and you talk about the state violence that was visited against people who were part of a movement, we have to agree that this violence had its impact. And the impact was on successive movements, where people said, "Well, I ain't crossing that line!" And we can even talk about it in the realm of culture. For example, think about Bob Marley. Think about how reggae made its fast transformation after Bob Marley. If you listen to him, and you listen to almost everybody after that with some exceptions, the trend of the music profoundly changed. Marley was a revolutionary artist.

Marc: And that was because Bob Marley had a commitment to challenging empire, which goes to my third point. You got the youth. You got the ethic of risk. But effective Black leadership also requires us to start challenging empire. When Martin Luther King stands up and says that there's a military industrial complex, when he starts talking about the relationship between global war and global poverty, when he starts talking about these intersectional forms of power and oppression, now his project is something bigger. So when I think about Black leadership at this moment, that's what I don't see enough. I see older leaders, I see leaders who aren't willing to take a risk, and I see leaders who are unwilling to challenge the real, fundamental power structure. It's like when Bill Cosby comes out and speaks against poor Black people. Even if some of his critiques were true, that's the easy part! The challenge of true leadership isn't picking on the vulnerable. As Michael Eric Dyson pointed out, don't go out and just challenge the poor kid on the block with his pants down low. Cosby would have had more credibility if he challenged NBC as well, and if he challenged those multinational corporations that paid his bills for all those years…

Mumia: …And then wouldn't let you buy the network!

Marc: Exactly! Courageous and visionary leadership requires you to take a stand and offer a critique when there's something at stake. Right now, we have a Black president who is endorsing crippling forms of global capitalism, prosecuting imperialist wars and failing to protect the most vulnerable citizens of the country. But so many Black leaders are content to be cheerleaders for the Obama Administration. Courageous and visionary leadership requires us to stand up and challenge him. And, of course, it's not "either-or," it's "both-and." We also have to protect the president from unjust and unfair assaults by those who aim to personally attack him, and, more importantly, to drag him even further to the political Right.

Mumia: True. So many of the things that Black leaders would say about George W. Bush or even Bill Clinton are not being said about President Obama. Yet they still apply! Poverty, war, civil rights, the environment—the list goes on. If we can't speak up right now, when are we gonna do it?

Courageous and visionary leadership requires you to take a STAND and offer a critique when there's something at stake.

Marc: Too many of us are content to sit at the "cool kids table." We don't want to challenge a Black president because it'll cost us some social capital, some book sales, some endorsement deals. We want to remain popular. After all, who doesn't wanna be popular? The problem is, racial justice ain't never popular. LGBT rights ain't never popular. If we are to be leaders and freedom fighters, rather than mere celebrities, then we must stand up and speak painful truths at moments of difficulty.

Mumia: Exactly. And that's a key part of your point about critiquing empire. Unless we have the courage and vision to point out how a president, even a Black one, is a part of the American empire, then our critique is lacking.

Marc: True. At the same time, there is a need for an internal critique. For a range of complicated reasons, Black people are engaged in some self-destructive behaviors, from using and selling crack and heroin to absentee parenting. How do we engage in the necessary work of collective self-criticism and taking responsibility without allowing that to become a red herring that distracts us from the structural issues that we've been pointing out?

Mumia: I agree with you, man, about the need for an internal critique. But I'm thinking it's got to be an *informed* critique, one that comes from a place of true understanding, as opposed to adding a whipping to those already whipped. From my vantage point, I see dudes, especially young bucks, who know nothing—*nothing*—about our folks' history. If they've been informed at all, it's been by their own somewhat truncated experience, and what's projected in the corporate press.

Marc: What you mean by that?

Mumia: Let me give you an example. I met a young buck here on The Row who was from North Philly. We used to talk during the one hour a day we're allowed outside our cells. I didn't know him, but his parents were about my age. In fact, he told me that his mom used to see me rolling down Columbia Avenue to the Panther Office. Anyway, he was up here in the yard rapping. Or trying to! He was saying some lyrics, like, "When I hit the bricks / I'ma be pimpin' thick / Flippin' them tricks..." So me and another older brother spoke to him when he finished, and asked him about all that pimp talk. Where did he get that stuff from? And you know where he got it from?

Marc: Where?

Mumia: He told us that he saw it in *The Mack*, the old movie with Max Julien. And when we asked why he was using the movie as a basis for reality, he said, "I saw the movie. Wasn't it like that back in the day?" I was shocked. I tried to tell him that it was only a movie, that real life pimps got mugged by dudes. Why? Because guys had sisters, aunts, friends and, after all, mama! I told him about dudes in my neighborhood that chased them with baseball bats. He saw a movie and he thought it was *real*. Too many people don't know because they've never been told. Or they grew up, perhaps separated from their parents and elders, and looked at movies, especially from the so-called Blaxploitation era, and thought these were more than entertainment. But to quote the Honorable Elijah Muhammad, "When you know better, you do better."

Marc: No doubt. And "knowing better" is the outgrowth of rigorous analysis, but also intergenerational dialogue. My generation cannot have a thorough understanding of the social landscape if elders aren't committed to engaging us, offering us their own counter-stories, and preparing us for the next stages of our struggle. And, of course, we have to be willing to listen with sincerity and humility!

Mumia: Both of us have mentioned Kanye West several times. Kanye just recently apologized to George W. Bush for calling him a racist in the wake of the Hurricane Katrina. But Kanye never actually called Bush a racist. He said, "Bush don't care about Black people." And if you looked at Katrina, I think that was a valid assessment.

Marc: Of course! We also have to find a way to sustain and encourage and protect those courageous voices so that they don't give in. Part of that is our responsibility.

Mumia: In addition to that protective force, the other thing is that you have to have independence. Today's leaders have none.

Marc: Well, from a historical perspective, one of the most free, protected and independent spaces for Black people has been the church. The Black church was never all political—you could even argue that it wasn't mostly political—but it was still a political base. In the current moment, however, how do you see the church's role in Black leadership?

Mumia: The present generation of Black church leadership, as it relates to the Black community, is frankly quite degraded from its historical antecedents. Du Bois makes the point that, unlike many people, our first real institution was not the family, at least not in terms of a legalized structure called marriage. It was the church. That was the only place where people could feel

Our first real institution was not the family, it was the CHURCH. We had to pray in hush harbors, in the field at two in the morning, but that's where our community began. The church should be the foundation of our organizing.

whole, human, loved and part of a broader community. It was either that or the fields, you dig? And even though we had to pray in secret, in hush harbors, in the field at two in the morning, that's where community began. So one would think that the church would be the foundation of every political organization among African-Americans within the last century. As you mentioned, what made it remarkable and made it the birthplace of many of our greatest leaders was precisely because it was independent.

Marc: Independence was really crucial, right? It was a free Black institution, for the most part. Of course, we could talk about its governing ideology and the ways that White supremacy operates within the context of the church. But in many respects it was free. Nowadays, most of our institutions are underwritten by private capital, which rarely represents our best interests. There are moments of convergence between their interests and ours, but fundamentally, these organizations aren't interested in producing strong leadership or enabling the rise of independent Black institutions. And I think this idea of being a free Black institution is critical for any type of leadership because you're not beholden to the government. You're not beholden to private capital. You have your own fundraising, your own leader. And you have your own vision. You have your own forms of tradition. You have your own forms of resistance.

Mumia: My statement of independence is far more than a sense of economic independence. By that, I mean spiritual independence. Psychological independence. I even mean cultural independence. And, of course, the farther we left the churches of the fields and the closer we came to Northern branches of those faiths and religious groups, the further from independence we became. The high water mark of church leadership might be that of Martin Luther King, Jr. as both a church leader and a Civil Rights leader. But as we've seen in the last half of the 20th century, and the beginning of the 21st, Black preachers are far less independent today than they were 40 years ago. And that's because of capital, on the one hand, and politics on the other.

Marc: You have these megachurch preachers with 16,000 parishioners— hell, a 6,000-member congregation is considered a small megachurch. And the preachers attached to them are literally bringing in tens of millions of dollars per year, easily. Shouldn't that make them more separate, more independent from these power structures?

Mumia: It would tend to make them want to think that. One would think that, yes, economically independent they would seem to be. But if you look at them and examine their rhetoric and look at their activities in the community, they are far more interlocked with political structures than, say, the Martin Luther King generation. I mean, think about Martin's wife, Coretta Scott King's, funeral. When you had two Bushes and both of the Clintons in a Black church.

Marc: Right. Right. And they're delivering votes to those people. Look at [First Baptist Church of Glenarden] in Maryland, where Pastor John Jenkins allowed President George W. Bush to speak from the pulpit, but refused to challenge his stance on affirmative action because he thought it was inappropriate. Think about all of the preachers who literally delivered votes to Bush in 2004.

Mumia: Right! And not only that, what did Bush do? He did something that was extraordinary: He created the Faith Based Initiatives. Or what I like to call the FBI!

Marc: Damn! I like that—the FBI. I never peeped that before!

Mumia: Well, it's real! He began to expend federal money on churches—in many cases, Black churches. And if I take your money, homie, you own me.

Marc: Right!

Mumia: So that's what I mean about independence. What you'll see are Black preachers talking about electoral politics around election time as though they're speaking for themselves or us. But they're essentially appendages of the Democratic Party and in some cases the Republican Party. What you won't hear is them talk about independent political power for Black people. Think about the 1972 National Black Political Convention in Gary, Indiana. People from all across the country came together and talked about the problems and possible solutions. Well, what were they going for? A politically independent Black Party to address the needs of African-Americans. We're no closer to that today than we were in 1972.

Marc: I agree. And I think so much of it is the fact that these Black institutions have been co-opted and corrupted. They have been fully infiltrated by market values, market logic and mainstream political ideologies. No longer are we trying to be revolutionary, or even radical. Early in Black life, there was nothing more radical than Sunday school literature. Even if we disagree with the Jesus piece or the adoption of a European religious tradition, the church was nonetheless used for resistance. And there are still spaces for that, whether they're within the Unitarian movements, Black branches of the United Church of Christ, or other Black radical churches that operate in the James Cone tradition of liberation theology. These churches have refused to become fundamentalist in their reading of scripture, a position that has never worked in favor of marginalized people. They've also managed to hold on to the "love ethic" of Jesus as the model for how we navigate the world and deal with social dilemmas. But, in general, many of our churches have adopted market logic. Even this idea of a gospel of prosperity, whereby your faith is measured by wealth—and not just your personal wealth but the wealth of your preacher—becomes a reflection of how the market has become the arbiter of Black cultural and religious and political life. The idea that these churches are basically neo-liberal, that our faith traditions have become neo-liberal, suggests that there's no space for radical political leadership in those places 'cause they have an unshakeable belief in capitalism. They believe that capitalism will not only free us politically, but spiritually. This is literally what cats like Creflo Dollar and Eddie Long say! That is a very strange space to occupy.

Mumia: If you analyze it philosophically and you look at the impact of say, Max Weber, on capitalism and the Protestant ethic, the same sensibility emerges.

Marc: Right. That's an important point of reference, as it shows how this sensibility isn't indigenous to Black religious life, but part of a much longer historical trajectory within the West.

Mumia: Absolutely. And African-American Christians and church leaders have taken that sensibility one step further. You know, Weber praised the Protestant ethic as a kind of capitalist model. In essence, he was an exemplar of the idea that the good Protestant didn't waste his time in idleness, but in productive—as in profitable—labor. The acquisition of wealth was a mark of one's faith in the divine. It was also God's measure of your goodness, your holiness. It was the spiritual foundation of Yankee profiteering. When you look at American history, getting money ain't just a hip-hop cliché—it's the very essence of the Protestant ethic. But these preachers are saying that your salvation can literally be measured by your wealth, right?

Marc: Right.

Mumia: Because your prosperity is a mark and reflection of your faith. You know, we come from people who came to church in rags. With no shoes, right?

Marc: Teach!

Mumia: With welts from whips on their backs. But their faith was more authentic and more real than the people who were whipping them, the people who were oppressing them, and the people who so-called owned them. These were people who acted, who survived, because of their faith. And we see the exact opposite of that today. Because even though we are in America, and I never want to forget this, among the richest Black tribe in the world—

Marc: —right. That ain't saying much, but you're right!

Mumia: —Our lives are a disaster! To quote Young Jeezy, "We livin' in hell!" Let's not fake this thing.

Marc: That's real. And that's my frustration with Black religious leadership. Too often, they're not drawing from a prophetic tradition. I don't care what your religious tradition is. You can, on some level, marshal it in the service of justice and freedom. But if you start to buy into the idea that people who are unsuccessful, simply don't work hard enough, that gays and lesbians aren't full human beings, that private greed is better than the public good, then we're no better than any other tradition. There have always been Black conservatives in the church. There have always been Black opportunists in the church. We had Sweet Daddy Grace. We had Father Divine. We had Reverend Ike. We had people selling luck 100 years ago. But they've moved from the margins to the mainstream, and now they're moving from the mainstream to the White House. These preachers get a little bit of access, they get a little bit of power, and suddenly they become proxies and agents for the radical Right Wing. And I'm not trying to suggest that their politics are completely inauthentic. Some of them really just don't believe in liberal politics, particularly on social issues. Black people are often quite conservative. I get that. But it seems to me that now there's little or no space for resistance. That notion of independence that you talked about—being divorced from these institutions, being separate from Washington, being separate from Wall Street—those are critical parts of a Black church. And it seems to me that we no longer want to speak back to Pharaoh. We're just happy to be sitting next to him.

Mumia: But Marc, it's actually worse than that, in my opinion. You know, none of us can escape our history, individually or collectively, as a nation or in this world. And what they have really done with the adoption of this kind of market-faith psychology is betray their history. Because if you praise the market enough, you will look back and you will find that you're now in the shoes of the slave master. You see, because he believed that everything was for sale. Even your mama!

Marc: Right! Exactly!

Mumia: And the Black liberation faith that kept our people sane and alive held that there are some things that can never be bought, that were beyond the market. A human being, for example. A child. We have betrayed that. If the market is all things, then human life and human dignity and human liberation mean nothing. They have no value.

Marc: Another place that we're beginning to see Black leadership emerge, at least ostensibly, is in the academy. Of course, we have always had Black intellectuals in leadership positions, most notably the great W.E.B. Du Bois. But now, some of the most visible faces within the Black public sphere are those of Michael Eric Dyson, Melissa Harris-Perry, Cornel West and, of course, Skip Gates. These folks are household names. As someone who operates from outside the academy, how do you see the role of the Black intellectual these days?

Mumia: Many of the people who you named are, of course, exceptions to the general rule. In fact, they're kind of seen as insurgents in academia. Think about how Harvard, one of the most prestigious universities in America, essentially kicked Cornel West to the curb because he was both a scholar and a cultural worker who combined brilliant academic analysis with music. And the elite of the university said that this was unprofessional.

Marc: Right. And, of course, Cornel was a tenured university professor, so they couldn't fire him. Instead, Larry Summers, who was president of the university at the time, came to him and questioned the legitimacy of his non-academic projects, as well as his support for the 2004 presidential campaign of Al Sharpton.

Mumia: Exactly. So one of the most brilliant minds of his generation is essentially disciplined for being too brilliant. For being academically and intellectually brilliant, but also for being a culturally brilliant person who contributes on another level. You know, most of what Cornel writes is not going to be read in the mainstream African-American community. But if he creates something like a piece of music, it will reach people who would not read one of his books, initially. But they might be turned on by the vibrations and say, "Damn this dude is bad. Let me check that book out!" So Cornel is disciplined for going outside of a narrow range of acceptable work. This really makes no sense at all because it's all life and it's all cultural work, is it not?

Marc: I agree man! And I think the idea that the intellectual has to operate in different spaces and engage different publics is a critical one. And I think in the past two decades, we've begun to see the effectiveness of that approach. For example, Cornel West can write *Race Matters*, which becomes a bestseller because he didn't just write for an audience of 20 academics. And then he does stuff with music that attempts to reach an even wider audience. I think that's a great

Some who are public intellectuals are more PUBLIC than they are intellectual.

idea. And when you see those of us who operate on TV, write popular books and have newspaper columns, I think we all have the potential to make powerful interventions in public life. Still, I'm concerned that some of us public intellectuals are more public than we are intellectual, and some of us aren't doing the work that really matters anymore, you know?

Mumia: That's a valid critique because TV can capture and then corrupt far more than it can enlighten. That means that those people who are doing that work have to be challenged, and I don't mean by their academic superiors. I mean by their people. You dig? By the people who consume their work.

Marc: Right.

Mumia: You know, I wrote a piece quite a few years ago that was designed to urge revolutionary intellectuals to become part of a collective. But the academy creates this kind of individual who stands alone and above the people. None of us is an island. We are all part of a collective. Plus the very reason that many of us exist in the academic arena is that a big collective called the Black Power Movement said, "Yo!" and demanded their presence. So to ignore the collective that put them in there is, well, jive. Can I still say jive?

Marc: I like "jive." Let's take it back to the '60s, dog! But you're right! There's an ethos in the university that promotes a kind of individualism over the collective in terms of how you get tenure, in terms of how you do your work. On top of that, the academy also promotes this notion of celebrity, so that you're actually encouraged to become a so-called star in your area of expertise. As a result, you're not necessarily thinking about a collective project anymore. And for a few of us, the so-called stardom isn't limited to the academy anymore. So cats ain't just thinking about tenure and promotion; they're thinking about their next book or movie deal. I mean, there's money out here to be made. And cats are trying to get it now. They're hustling just like anybody else.

Mumia: But who does that serve? Because if you're part of a collective, first of all, you're thinking about someone other than yourself. You're thinking about your people, or at least you're thinking about your class, right? And that promotes another kind of thinking, a broader kind of thinking so that your analysis begins to serve a social project. It's not about the Ivory Tower. It's about the communal and the collective, the broader sense of what self is. And therefore, if we admit that Blacks and women and gays and other people entered this arena because of a popular struggle, then you have to respond to the popular struggle that brought you.

Marc: Exactly! And some people would argue—and I'm starting to think that this might be the truth even though it might make me a hypocrite—that the most important and radical work that we can do as intellectuals won't happen as members of universities. I mean, if we're talking about leadership, then maybe intellectual leadership doesn't have to manifest that way. Think about White intellectuals throughout the 20th century, particularly the New York intellectuals of the 1950s. They were in salons. They were in coffee shops. They were writing for newspapers. They weren't working for a major research university and they weren't writing to university presses. They were writing to the people. Even in the Black power movement, much of the intellectual leadership that we had didn't come from universities.

Mumia: It came from the movement.

Marc: Right!

Mumia: But even before then, look at Du Bois. Here was a cat who essentially betrayed his class, betrayed his color in a sense—his high yellowness if you will—and devoted his life intellectually, artistically and politically to his people's struggle, and to a class struggle. Here was a man who denounced his citizenship because he found that he was more at home in Africa, in Ghana. You dig what I'm saying? And that's like almost unthinkable today, is it not?

Marc: You're right.

Mumia: And you know, people forget that Du Bois was on the board of directors of Black Swan, one of the first independent Black record companies.

Marc: Wow. I didn't know that.

Mumia: Oh yeah! I read about it in Angela Davis's book on blues women. But think about his impact culturally. If you read *The Souls of Black Folk*, he has a brilliant polemical work, but it's also art like a muthafucka. The poetry of it. The songs. Here's a person who is deeply inspired by the creative energy of his people. So you don't see the dichotomy between this brilliant intellectual, which he certainly was, and someone who captured in his spirit the sorrow songs of his people. But you know, my favorite Du Bois book isn't The *Souls of Black Folk*, it's *Darkwater*, which is far rougher and harder and angrier. But when you read his stuff, boy, you feel it.

Marc: That's one of the interesting things about Du Bois, and I think most people have him wrong. Most bourgeois Black scholars have sort of framed Du Bois as a bourgeois intellectual who was unabashedly elitist, who was detached from the people, and who possessed an almost blind optimism about the possibilities of American democracy in ways that blinded him to the realities of the world. Our dear brother Cornel West, to some extent, talks about Du Bois in that way in his essay "Black Strivings in a Twilight Civilization," where he references Du Bois's "Enlightenment optimism." I think other people, like Adolph Reed and Anthony Monteiro, are more accurate when they say that Du Bois was with the people. Du Bois was on the ground. He had a consistent belief in the necessity of collective struggle and collective economics. Du Bois had a thorough critique of American empire and he understood the interconnectedness of race and gender and class and power. And to me, that's the correct model of engaged Black intellectual leadership.

Edward Said talks about this idea of being in exile. And when I think about the work that we do as intellectuals, I don't care if you're in the academy or not, I think we have to take on a kind of self-imposed marginality, a self-imposed exile. So that even if you're *in* the university, you're not *of* it. But also, even if you're outside the university, you don't have its sensibilities governing how you write. I mean, in your case, you're an intellectual who's writing in literal exile, right? I won't go so far as to say that your circumstance is easier, but it certainly makes it more clear what the project is and what the stakes are. You have no doubt about what you're dealing with. But, man, I think a lot of cats start to think that because they're at Harvard or Yale or Columbia or wherever, that this shit can actually work out! They start to think that it's not a real struggle so they start going for self. If there's a failure of leadership from our intellectuals, it's that our intellectuals now want to be celebrity intellectuals rather than public intellectuals. And, look, I fall victim to that too. Shit, I got a TV show! You know what I'm saying?

Mumia: Right! Well, we all have models, no matter who we are. But when I look at models in terms of intellectuals, I can't get away from Du Bois. I can't get away from Angela Y. Davis. You dig? And these are people who, you know, walked it and talked it, and in many ways are still walking and talking. Even though Du Bois is not with us, to read his work today is to feel the power of his analysis.

Marc: Yes! *The Philadelphia Negro* still matters when we think about urban sociological analysis! *Black Reconstruction* still provides brilliant analysis of labor relations, of the political economy of war, of the psychological investment in Whiteness, education…

Mumia: And how many people are creating works that will last this way? How many people are producing work that folks will read 50 years from now and say, "*Got-damn!* I feel that!"

Marc: Not too many. But that's what I'm talking about!

Mumia: That's what it's about! 'Cause if it ain't about that, what's it about? It's never about the university. The university is a site. The university is a site for resistance, certainly. But it ain't home. You know, Du Bois wasn't home nowhere. Fisk gave him something, but you know University of Pennsylvania was like, *"Uh, you got about two minutes to get your Black ass outta here!"*

Marc: They gave him a broom closet.

Mumia: *"You brilliant, but you still a nigga!"* You dig what I'm saying?

Marc: No doubt. And I'm glad you mentioned Angela Y. Davis as a key leader, as so many of us will discuss Black leadership without ever invoking the name of a woman. In fact, in each of the areas we've discussed—

mainstream activist communities, Black churches, and the academy—there is a clear lack of female leadership. Clearly it's not because sisters aren't capable or willing, since each of these spaces has always been filled with brilliant, courageous and committed Black women. So how do we account for the stunning lack of female representation in leadership circles?

Mumia: Well, Marc, in my mind it's similar to your earlier critique of how older brothers didn't make room for younger leaders. They also didn't make room for sisters. That's really problematic, 'cause in each of the areas you've mentioned—activist communities, churches and the academy—who are the people in the body of these structures? Women. When I wrote *We Want Freedom*, I went back and read Bobby Seale's work, and I was actually quite surprised to find that he said that the majority of Black Panthers were women. That wasn't my recollection, but I only worked in three or four chapters and branches across the country.

We must prioritize GENDER equality as an indispensable part of any credible Black agenda.

Bobby, as chairman of the organization, certainly had a more informed view. I'd always thought that he meant to say that the most consistent and reliable members were sisters, because they showed up every day, rain, sleet or snow, and did the work. And that would certainly be true. They were the most conscientious, the most consistent, and in many ways, the most principled members and leaders. But, what about the church? Without Black women, what is the Black church but an empty building? And the same thing goes for these other institutions.

Marc: I agree. The fact that Black women demographically dominate these spaces yet have always had very little access to literal or representational power speaks to yet another perennial crisis of leadership. To me, this must be addressed in three ways. First, we must prioritize gender equality as an indispensable part of any credible Black agenda. After all, there are no

Black people or poor people who are not simultaneously gendered, and navigating a world that has differential expectations, privileges, penalties and possibilities based on those gendered identities. Second, we must demand that leaders engage in a critical gender analysis, in addition to race and class, when dealing with Black issues. For example, we can't talk about the prison industrial complex without talking about its impact on Black female bodies. We can't talk about economic globalization without talking about the ways that it is creating public health crises that have disproportionate impact on Black women. And third, we must commit ourselves to nurturing and promoting and sustaining Black female leadership, so that women aren't merely represented by proxy, even by well-meaning progressive brothers.

Mumia: Well, the Party was unlike many of our contemporaries, for it stood alone in the appointment of a Black woman who held undisputed organizational—and indeed, paramilitary—power. Read Elaine Brown's *A Taste of Power,* Safiya Bukhari's *The War Before* or *Assata*, and you'll see it. But I think one of the problems of the movement, then, as now, is that so many dudes rose up from the church, which is strictly and profoundly patriarchal, thus they are ideologically and theologically conditioned to see women as subordinate, you dig me? But I want to go back, way back, to a cat who rose not from the church, but from the realm of activism and struggle. He was clear as crystal on the central role that women's equality and freedom played in the Black freedom struggle.

Marc: Frederick Douglass!

Mumia: Yes sir! Against catcalls and curses, Douglass openly and publicly supported the suffragist movements. He wrote, spoke, and attended such gatherings shortly after slavery, and called for women's right to vote. He extolled one of the slogans of the movement, which has a resonance and reason that we should bring alive again in our day: "Intelligence has no sex!"

Marc: One of the consistent arguments throughout history, from Black leaders, has been that gender is important, but secondary to race. They argue that White supremacy is the organizing force and logic of America, and that we must deal with the race question first. Afterward, they argue, issues of gender, sexuality, etcetera, can be addressed. What do you make of that position?

Mumia: Hmm. That's a good one, bro. But I think it's important to read and study the writing of Black feminist thinkers on this question. Quite a few years ago, I read, *Critical Race Feminism*, a compilation of essays mostly by Black feminist scholars about the way that the law treats Black women. In it, Adrien Wing wrote that the law tends to see Black women as an additive like this: woman and Black, like $1 + 1 = 2$. She argued that Black female experience is actually multiplicative, and thus not susceptible to the simplistic legal logic of additives. She saw it as woman and Black and working class, etc., or $1 \times 1 \times 1 = 1$. No part of a woman can, in a real life sense, be subtracted or divided, for she is a being of many facets. This results in a whole being—single and distinctive. That always made sense to me, because it revealed the limits of the law, its shortsightedness. How can you subtract something that is integral to your being? We must abandon the legal circumscriptions for the reality of multidimensionality of our being. I think that's especially so when we look at the organizing principles of White supremacy, which adds, subtracts, divides and excludes. It is built on the principle of divide and conquer. But what if we embrace our multidimensionality? Human beings are Black, White, Indian, gay, straight, working class, poor, project-born—the list

Are we not fundamentally human, with more SIMILARITES than differences?

goes on. Still, are we not fundamentally human, with more similarities than differences? Or do we continue to embrace the illogic foisted upon us by a system that seeks to keep as at each other's necks? That is our choice, man. We have to take on all questions, at the same time, from the perspective of our multidimensional realities, and work to bring forth a stronger, more inclusive whole that rejects the narrowness of an actually false notion of White and male supremacy.

Marc: Absolutely. And if we've properly learned the lessons of history, we will incorporate all of these factors into a new vision of leadership. This new vision must be inclusive, democratic, principled, courageous, and, most of all, animated by a deep love of all people. It's an uphill struggle to enact this vision, but it's the work we must do if want to truly redirect the destiny of our people towards freedom.

FOR YOUR LIBRARY

Betrayed, Houston Baker

A Taste of Power, Elaine Brown

The Crisis of the Negro Intellectual, Harold Cruse

The Souls of Black Folk, W.E.B. Du Bois

Uplifting the Race, Kevin Gaines

Breaking Bread, bell hooks, Cornel West

Transcending the Talented Tenth, Joy James

Holy Mavericks, Shayne Lee and Phillip Sinitiere

Watch This!, Jonathan Walton

Race Matters, Cornel West

Critical Race Feminism, Adrien Wing (ed.)

CHAPTER 5

Black Life in the Age of Incarceration

Frederic Jameson once wrote, "It is easier to imagine the end of the world than the end of capitalism." Given the unprecedented number of American citizens currently under the thumb of the criminal (in)justice system, a similar claim can be made about prisons. In this discussion, we spotlight the increasingly central role that the prison plays in our social imagination, particularly as it pertains to the destinies of Black, Brown and poor people in America. In addition to our analysis, we articulate a vision for prison abolition, a process by which the prison would no longer play a primary role in our society.

Marc: Obviously you have a unique perspective on prisons, having been inside of them for nearly three decades. How do you see the role of the prison as we enter the second decade of the 21st century?

Mumia: It's is more omnipresent than it has ever been in African-American history and life. Of course, we can talk about that in terms of raw numbers and percentages, but I think more powerful than even those

Prison is infused into Black popular CONSCIOUSNESS and culture.

indicators is how the prison is infused into Black popular consciousness and culture. Much of what we do now has its genesis in prison. Look at the young brothers whose pants are hangin' around their butts. That comes from prison because when dudes get busted, especially given certain kinds of cases, the first thing they do is take your belt.

Marc: Right.

Mumia: Without your belt, your shit starts sagging. And for dudes who have been in and out of jail, it becomes cool and comfortable to roll like that. Without us even being conscious of it, the jail impacts us: how we walk, how we roll, how we dress. And it certainly has impacted hip-hop culture, not just in terms of lyrics but in terms of fact. I mean, look at T.I., DMX and others who are in and out of prison. And we know that in New York, and other cities across the country, they had a police squad devoted to hip-hop artists.

Marc: Yes! I grew up during the incarceration era. So many of my friends, family and oldheads went to prison. When I wouldn't see someone for a

Prison became a regular part of my life. I knew I didn't WANT to go to prison, but I never thought that it was completely avoidable.

while, I just assumed they were locked up. It became a regular part of my life. I knew I didn't want to go to prison, but I never thought that it was completely avoidable.

Mumia: Your generation definitely has had to come to terms with prison in a whole different way. Given the role that it now plays in our world, it's unavoidable that it'll affect you in a different way. It shapes your consciousness, your dreams and your aspirations.

Marc: How did we get here? How do we get to a moment in history where the prison serves such a primary function? I mean, think about 1970, there were more than 200,000 Americans incarcerated. Now, three decades later, we have 2.5 million people incarcerated and some 7.7 million people who are under control of the criminal justice system. One in three Black men between the ages 20 and 28 is under some kind of criminal supervision. When you look at the number of people incarcerated in this nation, it dwarfs every other developed nation in the world. It even dwarfs apartheid-era South Africa. Our incarceration numbers are higher than Cuba, China, Iraq and Pakistan combined. The prison population in most countries, both the Third World nations and in other capitalist empires, is infinitesimal in comparison to the United States. So why does the prison matter so much to us? Why do you think the prison is such a primary mechanism of sorting, punishing and containing within our society?

Mumia: Well I think it's several things. When there were approximately 250,000 to 300,000 people in American prisons in the '70s, we talked about it as a sign of fascism. And we protested! I personally was outside of Angela Davis's jail protesting with a dozen other Panthers and other supporters. But to look at that then, and to look at this reality now, is stunning. Of course, you have to factor in the deindustrialization of most urban areas in America.

Marc: How does deindustrialization factor into this?

Mumia: While we are sometimes too conditioned to think that this rough economic reality for Black America—especially working class Black America—is our norm, that ain't necessarily so. In some eras, and in some places, Blacks had strong presences in the world of work; in Pittsburgh, in the steel mills; in, say, the Budd factory in Northeast Philadelphia; in Detroit, the epicenter of the auto industry, there were Black men and women with good gigs, who after years of labor struggle were making truly middle-class wages. And this with little more than a high school diploma! In many ways, those days are gone. Thanks in part to Clinton's North American Free Trade Agreement, such industries fled the States for nonunionized places like Mexico, Indonesia and China. Meanwhile, the prisons expanded and, in a sense, this represents the biggest job switch in modern-day history. As jobs were sold off and outsourced for millions of Blacks, jobs in the repression industry were ladled out to the rural areas. Prisons—their construction and maintenance, food and medical services, and so forth—became big business. But there's something else far more insidious, which Michelle Alexander, author of *The New Jim Crow*, touches on in her work. She says that the Black bourgeoisie made a deal with Democratic Party leadership. It was like, "You can do your thing as long as we can do our thing." And the Black bourgeoisie's thing was affirmative action. They said, *"We'll turn the other way when you produce crime bills and stuff."* And that's because they were thinking that, through affirmative action, their class status would be safe. But this isn't just about class, it's also about caste.

Marc: Now when you say caste, you're talking about a kind of permanent status, as opposed to class, which one can transcend through wealth accumulation or education. But when you talk about a racial caste system, you're talking about something like slavery, something that you can't work or behave your way out of. In this case, in this country, being Black increases your chances of being detained, arrested, charged, convicted, sentenced and executed more than any other racial group in the nation. Like Ira Glasser, longtime head of the ACLU, did before her, Alexander points out how criminalization affects housing, education, employment and voting rights in ways that mirror post-Civil War Jim Crow policies. And, like you said, many Blacks stood by and allowed these policies to take form because they believed in the mobilizing possibilities of their class position.

Mumia: You're absolutely correct. And class is malleable, believe it or not. There are now a handful of Black billionaires, something that was unthinkable 30 years ago. There are quite a number of millionaires in different fields. There are Blacks in professions that have been historically all-White. I mean, there's a Black U.S. president! But you know caste means that some things are not remediable. They're impervious to change. And that's how the state looks at Black people as a rule. We're an exception to every rule. There used to be written into the law "The Black Codes." They were struck down, but they're still here; they have a life all their own. In fact, they emerged after Reconstruction as a way around so-called Constitutional rights per the 13th, 14th and 15th Amendments. No matter what people said, when it came Black folks those rights didn't really apply. It was like that then and in many ways, still is. For example, look at the Clinton presidency where the Black bourgeoisie praised, defended and fought for him. They call him the first Black president, and that's true— for people of the middle class. But for working class and average people, his presidency was a time of hell. Not just economically, but also in terms of the prison industrial complex. There was an explosion of prisons during his presidency.

Marc: That connects, as you pointed out, to this Faustian bargain that the Black middle class has made with the State. Programs like affirmative action and other public policies allowed them to get better jobs, attend Ivy League universities, and obtain other mechanisms for class mobility. But as you pointed out, they turned a blind eye to the criminalization of Black people through other social policies. To me, the only way this can happen is if the Black bourgeoisie comes to believe that there are fundamental cultural and social differences between themselves and the Black poor.

Mumia: Well, Marc, I don't think they consciously go around thinking that. But class impacts consciousness. If you live at a pronounced spatial distance and income level from the vast majority of Black folks, after a while you'll begin to think differently. This happens in part because your experiences are different from the poor. Also, for people who have made that transition, especially at a relatively young age, they tend to imitate those who have made such a transition before them. In a sense, they model those who are presumed to be functioning in the appropriate manner. And guess what? White upper class dudes look down their noses at poor White folks. That's where that "trailer trash" thing comes from. For middle and upper income Blacks, it's no great leap to model that behavior and talk about "ghetto trash." Dig me? Also, they're runnin,' man. They don't want no parts of the post-industrial dystopia that Black working America has become. They want to escape that! They look at North Philly the same way Dickens looked at the slums of London in *A Tale of Two Cities*—separate and alien.

Marc: Right, and this leads to a deep sense of shame and embarrassment about the poor. These feelings then lead to the passive or active endorsement of policies that further alienate and humiliate the Black poor. And this is what I think people miss. It's not that more people are going to jail because they're more poorly behaved or because they're more committed to crime. No, our willingness to shame, contain and blame the Black poor have emboldened us to put a wider range of policies in place that shift and expand what it means to be a criminal.

Mumia: Well, it's actually deeper than that, Marc. Because when you look at cities like New Orleans or like Philadelphia during the 5 Squad era, and even afterward, you had police predation on Black communities. They were preying on the poor. And the poor had no one to defend their interests. No one. It took extraordinary efforts to begin to address that hellish situation.

Marc: No doubt. I was born in Philadelphia during the last stages of the Frank Rizzo era. I still hear the stories of how brutal many of those officers were. Hell, the police ran into our house before I was born and beat

The police ran into our house before I was born and BEAT my father unconscious after he had called them for help!

my father unconscious after he had called them for help! Still, I think that police predation, surveillance and repression can only happen in a widespread fashion if there's a commonsense belief that there's a "criminal element" and that this element can only be handled through enhanced police presence. For me, this comes back to public policy.

Mumia: Well, public policy creates criminals, doesn't it? That is to say, the "law" is what the rulers say the law is, right? How else can cops commit crimes—steal, loot and kill for years with complete impunity—unless the ruling class decided to look away? But I wouldn't call it a "commonsense belief," but projected belief that certain folks are inherently, indeed genetically, criminal. One hundred years ago, in the streets of cities like New York and Philadelphia, the WASP aristocracy was saying, writing and preaching the same things about what they called "Fenian subhumans," referring to the Irish. I remember reading how Irish dudes were in with

Blacks, Indians and others talking about, "those damned White people." Back then, "White" meant "English" or "British." It didn't mean them, the Irish–and no one thought it did. Were they a "criminal element?" If you read the daily or weekly papers, or the laws that were passed, the answer is "yes." That was long before the era of Black ascendancy.

Marc: I feel you, which is why I hold on to that notion of "commonsense." These aren't ideas that are being debated and ultimately accepted at a particular moment in history by the general public. People just understand things like criminality, punishment or the necessity of prisons to be true without any reflection. That's what sociologist Pierre Bourdieu would call a *doxa*. I think that the average American believes in the law with an almost religious fervor. As a result, they don't think about the ways in which the law is subjectively written and enforced in order to expand the space for criminality. The current laws that we have on the books produce more levels of criminalization within the schools, streets and communities. For example, a first-grade girl screams at her teacher and, instead of getting a detention like in the old days, she gets carried away in handcuffs for disorderly conduct. Of course you shouldn't scream at your teacher and you should be punished if you do, but the decision to criminalize the behavior is new. And dangerous. The so-called War on Drugs, which begins *before* there is a spike in American drug usage and

Law is what the rulers say it is. How else can cops commit crimes— stealing, looting and killing for years with IMPUNITY—unless the ruling class decided to look away?

before crack hits the streets, becomes a way to expand our commonsense definition of who and what is criminal. We've taken drug addiction, which is essentially a medical problem, and turned it into a criminal act.

At the end of the day, crime is a social construct. People commit *acts*, which are then deemed "crimes" at particular historical moments. Obviously, some of these acts, like rape or murder, should be deemed criminal and, more importantly, socially unacceptable. Other acts, however, have been arbitrarily reframed as crimes as part of ever-expanding technologies of the repressive state. These technologies enable the fortification of the prison industrial complex.

Mumia: Angela Davis made a critical point, perhaps more explicitly than any other scholar. She said that at the close of the Cold War, the American empire needed a new enemy. The enemy that they decided on and targeted was "criminality." And all the energies of this national security state were directed toward this new internal enemy. And who makes the best internal enemy? The Black folks who have been the eternal alien in this country, of course.

Marc: Exactly. And, in my estimation, this happens through two strategies: the *creation* of laws that disproportionately affect Black people and the *enforcement* of laws that disproportionately affect Black people.

The current laws produce more levels of criminalization within our communities. For example, a first-grader screams at her teacher and, instead of getting a detention, she gets carried away in HANDCUFFS.

Mumia: Yes. And while that has changed for the bourgeoisie, it is still that way for poor and working class Black people. They live in the midst of a criminalization factory.

Marc: And this hasn't been the case for poor Whites.

Mumia: Nope. Anyone who's studied American history or seen movies like *Gangs of New York* knows that gangs have been here as long as there have been cities, and as long as there have been Americans. When New York was a White and Irish town, they had gang wars that would make the Crips and Bloods tremble. With names like the Bleeders, the Deathfetchers and the Killers, they were notorious for their rumbles, rapes and robberies, though mostly their use of arson against enemies. But you didn't see that kind of criminalization. I learned by reading Noel Ignatiev's book—

Marc: —*How the Irish Became White.*

Mumia: Right. From *How the Irish Became White*, I learned how one day this gang was doing what gangs do—rape, rob and fight. And then next day they put uniforms on them and they were the police department. Just like that. And this is New York City!

Marc: Damn! And that's what's so interesting. I think that's part of the work of intellectuals and activists: to put a spotlight on the complexities of this prison circumstance. Because people think about the prison crisis, if they're even willing to call it a crisis, in ways that assume people are just committing crimes. But what they often don't understand is that the very notion of crime is historically specific and socially constructed; it shifts across time and space. Like you said, we've always had gangs but we only develop a so-called gang crisis when it's colored folk in the gangs. Or when you look at drug use, Blacks and Whites use cocaine at the same rate, but crack cocaine becomes criminalized in a way that powder cocaine doesn't because crack/powder usage is drawn along racial lines. This distinction is reified through the media propaganda machine, which spends a decade telling us that crack cocaine, the supposed poor Black drug, is more dangerous, causes instant addiction, is a bigger threat to pregnancy, and a million other lies that justify harsher penalties. The consequence, of course, is that poor Black cocaine users end up in prison, while White cocaine users get slaps on the wrist. Don't get me wrong; I ain't mad at that. After all, love, treatment and care is what Whites deserve if they're struggling with addiction. I just want some of that humane policy response for Shaniqua and Raheem too!

Mumia: Ain't that the truth! But when you check it out, really, it comes down to the criminalization of consciousness, dig me? In every society known to man, people have used substances to expand and elevate consciousness. Africans smoked iboga and saw their ancestors. Indians smoked locoweed to see visions. And millions of Europeans drank wine to see and experience the divine. They just called it "Mass"!

Marc: I never thought of it quite that way!

Mumia: Back in the '30s, a dude named Harry Anslinger used the threat of drugs to scare people into supporting harsh laws against drug usage. Of course, he also used racism by talking about drug-crazed Negroes who raped White women and Mexicans who ran through bullets. Now let's be real, this has got to be one of the most drug-addicted societies in world history. It's just that millions of folks used drugs that were licensed and legally prescribed through the legal drug pushing industries. So dudes and dudettes are cooked up on lithium, librium, Valium or Viagara. And if they get too baked, they go to Betty Ford to get flushed out. Meanwhile, Laquesha and Rosita go to Alderson Women's joint, or some other hardcore hellhole because they wanted to escape the hell of their lives. Now, who's got a better reason to escape, if only briefly? Laquesha or Betty? And all too frequently, the imprisonment process produces more negative effects than the damned addiction itself!

Marc: Absolutely. And we see similar practices happening in the realm of mental health. Look at what Reagan did in the 1980s. At the same time that he was closing down mental health facilities, some states were criminalizing panhandling, public drunkenness, public urination, and all these so-called anti-social behaviors. On its face, this may not seem like a big deal, but when you combine increased criminalization with decreased social resources, you end up with not only incarceration but *transcarceration*. You're basically transferring people from one social institution to another. The federal money that was going to mental institutions is now going to expand, among other things, the military state and the budding prison industry. The consequence, however, is that people with legitimate mental health issues are now thrown into prisons, where their issues are ignored and exacerbated because of the hellish conditions of prison. This only increases recidivism and threatens the safety of everyone. Nevertheless, we're at this historical moment where, against all sensible evidence to the contrary, we're committed to criminalization.

Mumia: Well, we live in a country that has its origins in the criminalization of belief and thought. I mean, think about the pilgrims. These were among the most narrow-minded people in American history because they exiled people whose beliefs differed one iota from the accepted belief. And that has been in the American psyche for literally hundreds of years, this idea of exclusion. I mean, you can't be more excluded and breathing than to be in an American prison, or any prison for that matter. But in American society, this is the eternal exclusion of citizens, where, for the most part, you cannot vote or meaningfully participate in civil society.

Marc: On top of that—and I know you've talked about this in your most recent book *Jailhouse Lawyers*—there's been a recent wave of laws that have further undermined the rights of prisoners while they're still incarcerated. For example, under the Clinton Administration, we saw the introduction of the Prison Litigation Reform Act (PLRA) and other laws that went under the public radar. What has been the scope and effect of these policy shifts?

Mumia: The PLRA, the Antiterrorism and Effective Death Penalty Act (AEDPA) of 1996—these laws were designed to literally shut and seal the courthouse doors to hundreds of thousands and ultimately millions of prisoners. So it becomes an obstacle course. Under the PLRA, prisoners were blocked from filing suits if they'd filed several before that had been dismissed. There were severe time limits on when we could file as well as limitations on damages and attorney's fees! Now if you know anything about a lawyer, you know that if you limit or cap his fees, you've essentially taken a blowtorch and welded up his client's prison doors, dig me? The AEDPA did essentially the same thing with *habeas corpus* laws. It essentially was passed because so many dudes was winning their cases!

For real. These laws are not based on the predication that unconstitutional things aren't happening to American citizens in American prisons. It's, *"We don't want you to sue nobody."*

Marc: Right! Basically, *"Y'all are winning too much so we'll change the rules of the game!"*

Mumia: You change the problem; you change the remedy. And with the PLRA, as I wrote in *Jailhouse Lawyers*, it was based on nothing but lies.

Marc: Lies and distortions, like the idea that a prisoner sued because the prison didn't have a salad bar.

Mumia: Yeah. Or that someone was suing about peanut butter: *"He ordered creamy and he got chunky."*

Marc: Exactly. In each case, prisoners were suing for serious issues, yet they were dismissed and turned into something frivolous. In *Jailhouse Lawyers* you explained how the salad bar was actually one part of a 27-page complaint about a range of problems, including unhealthy ventilation, overcrowding, rodents, failure to segregate prisoners with contagious diseases, and a complete absence of nutritious foods. The salad bar was merely one of many suggestions that the petitioner offered for fixing the circumstance. And the peanut butter complaint was actually about prisoners systematically being charged for goods that they never received. Sadly, there's little space to discuss the rights of prisoners with a presumption of dignity and legitimacy.

Mumia: And Judge Jon O. Newman of the Federal Court of Appeals Second Circuit ordered these cases from his circuit. He read the cases and was like, *"This isn't about abuses at all. You guys aren't telling the truth."* But really, I think it comes down to the media and not just radical lefties. It has to break through mainstream media. That's the tool that they use to promote the agenda. I remember clear as a bell when the case was on "20/20" and they were like, *"Can you believe this prisoner sued because he didn't get chunky peanut butter? More stories coming up next!"* But it was

BS. And no reporter really researched it. Next thing you know, you got a groundswell of people saying, *"Well, you need to change these laws! All these prisoners in there talking about peanut butter!"*

Marc: Right. And that's the same strategy used for welfare reform. The media began to proliferate stories of the "welfare queen," a lazy, immoral, hypersexual Black woman who was bilking the system for cash. By framing welfare as a handout to poor Blacks, who are marked as undeserving of social supports, it's easy to create public animus toward the welfare state. Why? Because Black misery is tolerable in this country. With prisoners, the framing is even easier. While most people on welfare are not Black—they're White, female and young—the prison population actually is predominated by Black and Brown bodies. On top of that, our collective disposition toward the "criminal element" allows us to demonize and dehumanize people who break laws, such that people believe that terms like "prisoner rights" are oxymoronic.

Mumia: It shows you the role and the function of the media in transforming social consciousness, and then transforming policies always to the detriment of the people. I mean, think of it this way. If they can sell us a war against a people who didn't do nothin' to us, then what about fear? George H.W. Bush became president of the United States because he used the specter of a Black rapist, Willie Horton, to scare White folks, especially White women, into voting for him. Clinton stole some of his thunder. In essence, he sold Americans the prison as a late capitalist jobs program, or a jobs program for Bubbas in America's rural districts. Worked like a charm! The sell became easier as the media convinced us that drugs were a Black problem, even though more drug dealers and users were White. Prison became a "natural" solution.

Marc: We've been talking about how the prison is firmly positioned in the American public imagination. And we've talked about the policy dimensions of it. So what do we do? What should the goal of our prison activism be? There are some people who believe that prison reform is the key; that we need to change prisons and fight for human rights in prisons. And then there are those of us who take a far more radical approach and say that we need to actually get rid of prisons. What do you say to those who say that prison *abolition* is the goal?

Mumia: Well, you can guess where my position comes down on that continuum, right? The question of abolition is a radical position to be sure, but one that is presented by someone who is perhaps best positioned to present that argument. I speak here, of course, about dear Angela Davis, who wrote the book, *Are Prisons Obsolete?* And, if I may, I wanted to just take a moment to read her observation:

"When I first became involved in anti-prison activism during the late 1960s, I was astounded to learn that there were then close to 200,000 people in prison. Had anyone told me that in three decades, 10 times as many people would be locked away in cages, I would have been absolutely incredulous. I imagine I would have responded something like this: As racist and undemocratic as this country may be, remember during this period the demands of the Civil Rights movement had not yet been consolidated, I do not believe that the U.S. government would be able to lock up so many people without producing powerful public resistance. No, this will never happen. Not unless this country plunges into fascism."

Marc: That hits the nail right on the head. And the fact that prisons can become so normalized in our imaginations over a period of 30 years speaks to just how powerful the political and ideological machinery of the State has been. The only way you can lock up millions of citizens without having civil unrest is if you make people believe that there's a moral and civic crisis that can only be redressed through mass incarceration. So we start a so-called War on Drugs, or we have these wars on crime, or we have these wars against gangs, and so on and so forth, to ostensibly solve problems. But the fact is that the crime rate isn't really any higher now than is was before. If prison expansion were paralleling the expansion of crime, these policies would make sense. But the fact is that even when crime is down, prison construction and occupation are growing.

Mumia: That's right.

Marc: And so it seems to me that if we're going to talk about prison abolition, we need to talk about two things. First, we need to talk about *de-carceration*, finding ways to get people out of prisons. Whether it's getting rid of the money bail system, pre-trial detention, or allowing for the early release of non-dangerous prisoners, we have to find ways of getting people out of cages and back into society where they can become productive citizens. But more importantly, we must also engage *ex-carceration*, the idea of getting rid of incarceration as the primary or even secondary method of responding to crime. If we were to decriminalize victimless crimes, like personal possession of marijuana, prostitution or gambling, we would immediately knock a huge chunk of the prison population out right away, without any corresponding increase in crimes. If we were to treat drug addiction as a medical rather than criminal problem, we would create healthier and safer communities. If we were to provide proper mental health facilities, we could shrink the prison population by pre-emptively addressing criminality and by placing many current prisoners in the appropriate space to address their problems. We should also begin to find alternative responses to incarceration, such as community dispute resolution, restitution, suspended sentences and community probation. Ultimately, it seems to me that if we wanted to, we could empty out the bulk of prisons without endangering society at all. To me, that's the key to an abolitionist position: recognizing that it is both possible and socially beneficial to have a world without prisons.

Mumia: You know it's certainly a valid and interesting notion. I've often wondered what would a parallel universe look like that didn't have these kinds of things. And we actually have one that we can examine fairly close as Americans; we can go North and look at Canada. You don't see anything close to the kind of madness and fever for incarceration in Canada that we do in the United States. So we must conclude that there is another variable that's flipping the numbers. For me the only variable that works is race, the African-American presence in this country that is far more diminished in that country. They say we're 13 percent of the U.S. population. I happen to think that we are considerably more, but even if you say that it's 13 percent, that's a considerable number. There's nothing close to that in Canada, you see. And I think that has to explain why you don't have that explosion in prisons.

Marc: That's an interesting point, but I would push back a little bit. On the one hand, it's undeniable that Black folk are catching the most hell and that Black folk are overrepresented in the prisons. There's just no population of people who are even close. Latinos don't have it good—their incarceration rates are absurd as well—but Black men and women are dealing with slavery-era levels of bondage. I get that. But it seems to me that there's a broader framework that is less about race and more about poverty. To me, the overarching frame within the American context is what sociologist Loïc Wacquant calls the "carceral management of poverty," where prisons became a key mechanism of social control. Social phenomena like unemployment and homelessness become managed through incarceration rather than the expansion of social programs and opportunities.

Mumia: I wouldn't disagree with you. I would, in fact, agree and say that when you look at the levels of poverty in the African-American community, you have a perfect correlation.

Marc: Right. And I think that race becomes one of the primary mechanisms that this class antagonism plays out, 'cause you couldn't have Black bodies caged in if you don't have a class defending State to begin with. So at that level I think race and class operate together. For example, in New York, they've decriminalized marijuana possession as long as it's less than 25 grams and not in "plain view." This seems like a good idea, but becomes problematic when you look at how the city's "stop and frisk" policy disproportionately targets Black males. Our constitutional rights are violated as we're subjected to illegal searches that result in us getting charged, or really overcharged, with felony possession with intent to sell. Because most of us don't have the economic resources to fight the charges and win, we end up pleading to a lesser charge and becoming part of a criminal justice system that undermines our chances at housing, education and employment. This is something that would never happen in spaces of privilege. For God's sake, imagine if the police invaded the campus of Harvard, Princeton or Columbia University on any given Friday night. How much drug possession, public drunkenness and public urination would you find? Enough to justify the construction a whole new set of prisons! But they ain't looking there. And targeting is key. This is why 70 percent of New York's prisoners come from only three counties and seven distinct neighborhoods, research we have because it was done by prisoners at Greenhaven Correctional Facility in New York in the late 1980s. Because those folk are being targeted and they don't have the economic resources to get justice. Now, of course, the point you once made to me is critical too, which is that Black folk with money still end up not getting the same type of justice as White folk. That's what made the O.J. Simpson trial and verdict so spectacular. For the first time, a Negro got the kind of so-called justice that rich White people get.

Mumia: That's right. That's right. Well, you know, he had extraordinary resources and if published accounts are to be believed, he spent upwards of $4 million on his defense. And we recall that one of his lawyers was a law professor from a major law school in the state. This ain't the kind of stuff you get appointed when you come into an office and say, "Hey, I need a lawyer."

Marc: You get somebody fresh out of law school who, regardless of their intentions, simply can't give the kind of zealous defense that money affords. Now, let me ask you a question with regard to this abolition thing because this is something I struggle with: What do we do with the rapists, the serial killers and the child molesters? If we're trying to imagine a world without prisons, what do we do with people who are serious threats to society? 'Cause those aren't poverty-based crimes. Those crimes aren't reducible to mere social inequality.

Mumia: I can accept that. But if we continue doing what we've been doing, we have to address the fact that prisons are criminogenic. That is, they create and spark criminality in people who are otherwise not so inclined. So you're creating rapists and others of that ilk because they come to prison to get educated about crime.

Marc: Fair enough.

Mumia: Second, this kind of twisted thinking comes from our society, which profoundly devalues women and devalues life. So society teaches that some lives are valuable and some lives aren't. And it teaches us how to respond to that.

Marc: Right. But what do we say to the pragmatic question of, "What do we do with social outcasts who are a threat to society?"

Mumia: We treat them like human beings and we do what countries all over the world do. We work with them and we treat them. Some people have psychosis. We bring them out of that psychosis. But if we deal with them like human beings, we can expect human results from that process.

Marc: I agree. And, for me, this may in fact require some form of voluntary or forced confinement. In my opinion, this doesn't contradict the premise of prison abolition, which is to eliminate the prison as the predominant site of resolution, placement and containment. As an abolitionist, I don't disagree that there are people who need to be taken out of society because they are a social danger. But prison can too often become an easy solution to a complex problem. Instead of healing the individual, or addressing the fundamental social issues that helped to produce that individual, we simply lock people in cages for long periods of time. Let me ask you another question. In light of everything that we're confronting—racism, poverty, neoliberalism and all the ideological apparatuses of the State—what can we do right now to reverse the current trend of mass incarceration? How can we effect change, however small, in the immediate future and in the long term?

Mumia: Well, Marc, in the immediate future we have to acknowledge that change is happening, if only for the wrong reasons—because of the falling economic conditions confronting those American states that carry the biggest correctional burden in the United States. What that means, concretely, is that the vast majority of states are decarcerating dudes in order to cut their budgets. Long term, though, we have a problem, especially in the absence of a real, broad and deep abolition movement. I think folks are beginning to dare to think those thoughts that were taboo just a little while ago: abolition! But, absent a movement, I don't see it happening because politicians and the media will easily play the fear tape. But ultimately, the contradictions of the past have a way of creeping into our present. For me, that means that the Black bourgeoisie will have to learn from its distant and recent past to understand that their self-interest lies in creating a system that doesn't have the hunger it has to devour and destroy Black life. I'm thinking about Frederick Douglass, right after the

Instead of healing the individual, or ADDRESSING the fundamental social issues that helped to produce that individual, we simply lock people in cages for long periods of time.

Civil War, when all the old abolitionists were putting down their placards, shutting their Bibles and marching home like saints going to glory. In essence, he said, *"Hold up! Hold up! This thing ain't over."* They ignored him, of course, but the old man, perhaps the finest Black leader of his and many successive generations, had a million brilliant insights. Douglass said, "Slavery has been fruitful in giving itself names. It has been called the 'peculiar institution,' the 'social system' and the 'impediment' … It has been called by a great many names, and it will call itself by yet another name; and you and I will and all of us had better wait and see what new form this old monster will assume, in what new skin this old snake will come forth next." It seems to me that the old man had something there.

Marc: He definitely did. And I'm convinced that this monster is beatable. But, as you said, nothing is possible without a movement. We need to continue organizing ourselves on local, national and, yes, global levels. After all, the prison has not only become a staple of the domestic punishment industry, but is now being exported internationally through politico-military sites of repression like Guantanamo Bay and Abu Ghraib. Like Martin Luther King did, we have to spotlight those connections between race, poverty and militarism. Also, although abolition is our goal, we must also fight for immediate prison reforms, as long as they don't reinforce the idea that prisons are ultimately a viable institution. For example, fighting for proper medical treatment or protection from physical abuse for the currently incarcerated has to be a part of our goal too. But this fight has to be understood as bridgework toward abolition. It must be accompanied by a very clear and unshakeable critique of prisons as inevitable sites of state-sanctioned containment and violence. Otherwise, we run the risk, even through our well-intentioned, courageous and principled activism, of reinforcing the falsely obvious idea that prisons can be "fixed." The other piece of this is pedagogical. In other words, we have to teach the world how to understand a world without prisons. This means that as teachers, writers, activists and other cultural workers, we need to continue to challenge the unjust dimensions of the punishment industry. We need to spotlight the relationships between mass incarceration and issues of race, class, gender and empire. Finally, and most fundamentally, we have to begin to raise questions about the role, purpose and function of punishment in our society. We have to ask what it means to live in a world that equates justice with punishment and punishment with confinement. What are the other possibilities? Once we begin to do this work, people will be empowered to raise critical questions and offer new possibilities. We will be able to imagine a world "that is not yet."

FOR YOUR LIBRARY

Jailhouse Lawyers, **Mumia Abu-Jamal**

The New Jim Crow, **Michelle Alexander**

Are Prisons Obsolete? **and** *If They Come in the Morning*,
Angela Y. Davis

Discipline and Punish, **Michel Foucault**

Downsizing Prisons, **Michael Jacobson**

The Rise of the Penitentiary, **Adam Jay Hirsch**

States of Confinement, **Joy James, ed.**

Race to Incarcerate, **Marc Mauer**

Marked, **Devah Pager**

Instead of Prisons, **Prison Research Education Action**

Crack in America, **Craig Reinarman and Harry G. Levine, eds.**

Lies, Damned Lies, and Drug War Statistics, **Matthew B. Robinson
and Renee G. Scherlen**

Forced Passages, **Dylan Rodriguez**

Punishing the Poor, **Loic Wacquant**

CHAPTER 6

They Schools: Education and Its Discontents

From the moment African people arrived on American shores, we have envisioned education as a pathway to freedom. Our struggles for literacy, access to schooling and desegregation have all been animated by a belief that quality education would bring us closer to gainful employment, full citizenship and humane treatment. In recent years, however, schools have not only failed to meet our collective needs, but have become sites of miseducation, repression, and preparation for the prison industrial complex. In this conversation we examine the current education crisis and its connection to broader social, cultural and economic issues. We also attempt to reimagine education and schooling in ways that lead to true learning, consciousness and liberation.

Marc: I've had the opportunity to read some of your unpublished writing, and one of the things that surprised me was how much you think about education. Right now we're in the midst of a national education crisis, yet somehow educational issues don't seem to get the same kind of attention as foreign policy, health care or the economy. What do you make of the current moment with regard to education?

Mumia: What we're seeing is a crisis on top of a crisis. That is to say that there's always been a crisis in African-American education. But I think it has gotten considerably and significantly worse, largely because of the No Child Left Behind Act, and now Race To The Top. What is happening now is the commodification of education. There used to be an accepted wisdom that education is a social good in and of itself, that it helps society and individuals. Not just because education allowed people to get jobs, but because it helped people perform better in a functioning democracy. I don't see that anymore. Now I see education as a store: those who have credit or money can purchase education. Those who don't, well, *"This ain't for you."* It reminds me of what George W. Bush used to say over and over again: "This is an ownership society." It took me a while to understand that Bush was speaking globally. He was talking specifically about Social Security and housing ideas, but he really meant everything. "This is an ownership society," which means that if you can't buy it, if you don't own it, then you have no say in it.

Marc: That's interesting. And I think you're right. I think that the logic of late capitalism—privatization, globalization and free-market fundamentalism—has extended to education. As you mentioned, education was once imagined as something that transcended the market. It was understood as a universal good. Now obviously, education was never truly a utopian project. At every moment in history, the distribution of educational resources and credentials has been linked to class and caste and the broader interests of the State. Still, education was at least proffered as an elixir for our social ills, as the catalyst for social mobility. Education was understood as the key to a perfected self and a perfected society. However romantic and naïve this Enlightenment ideal may have been, it at least allowed us to sustain a belief in the fundamental value of education. But now, education has been dumped into the same pile as every other dimension of social life, and is governed by the same technocratic logic as everything else. As a result, educational success, growth and efficiency are measured by standardized high stakes tests and profit margins. So ideas about citizenship, identity and critical thinking—and not critical thinking in the superficial sense, but really asking dangerous and counterintuitive questions about power relations within society—have become completely marginal within mainstream conversations on education. And that's really scary because the stakes are getting higher and higher as we confront record unemployment, mass incarceration and the spread of HIV/AIDS. We are really facing a crisis of democracy. More and more people have less and less say about what goes on in their lives. If anything, education should be of more value now than perhaps any other moment in history since slavery. Sadly, that's not the case.

Mumia: I can't help but feel that all of what we see when we talk about the "crisis in democracy" is that education has betrayed its function as the institution that teaches democracy, as well as science, literacy, and logic to

Americans. Why? Because so much of it is directed at Black Americans. And that ain't what it was designed to do, dig me?

Marc: That's interesting. Say more about what you mean by that.

Mumia: What I mean, man, is that since the 1954 *Brown v. Board of Education* decision where the Supreme Court outlawed segregation in public education in America, powerful social forces have tried to defeat it. But now it's by other means. So they have attacked education—as a citizenship right—by other routes. Defending it. Delegitimizing it. Damning teachers. Something insidious began with *Brown* and it ain't never stopped—massive resistance by White supremacists both in the South and the North to make *Brown* meaningless. As Americans we get all choked up about Martin Luther King on his Birthday, but if he saw how Black and brown kids are violated in U.S. schools today, he'd vomit!

Marc: He sure would. After all, Martin Luther King's commitment to integration had less to do with his belief in the fundamental value of racial diversity than his understanding that the nation would never tolerate second-class schools if White people were in them. *Brown* wasn't really about Black folk fighting to get access to White classmates. It's not like we thought our IQs would go up if we were sitting next to White kids. No, we thought books and teachers and other necessary resources would be there if schools were integrated. Why? Because the nation has always refused to tolerate white misery. We've always had to whiten the face of poverty for it to be real and urgent to the general public.

Mumia: That's for sure!

Marc: But now, we live in an era of aggressive *re-segregation* of schools in the post-Brown era. Since the 1980s, none of the branches of government have demonstrated any commitment to school integration. Courts stopped ordering, and in fact have begun to reverse, and even deny, desegregation plans. Little is being done to stop residential segregation. As a result, we're looking at schools that are just as segregated and underdeveloped as the ones we fought to integrate in the 1950s.

Mumia: Right, and this is just one of the ways that schools are being systematically attacked. But this one is fundamental because segregated schools only make it easier to ignore those "second-class schools" you mentioned.

I've never seen teachers talked about so VICIOUSLY as I have in the last four or five years.

Marc: Ignore, indeed. It's stunning how uninterested the public is with regard to issues of education. Think about the historic presidential election of 2008. We talked about health care to the point that everyday people knew what co-ops and public options were. We saw the same kind of thing with topics ranging from weapons of mass destruction to off-shore drilling. Still, in the midst of those debates and conversations, education got very little play. I mean, you can't become president without having a clear stance on tax policy, gay marriage, abortion, military diplomacy or the role of the free market. Yet, a clear and articulate stance on education, whatever it may be, is simply not a prerequisite for public office. As much scrutiny as we give to cabinet appointments, almost no one cares about who becomes secretary of education. What does this all mean?

Mumia: Well, I think there's a reason for it. It goes back to the no man's land in American politics, which is not just race but racism—specifically white supremacy. And when you talk about education in the main, what you're talking about is public education, and that affects overwhelmingly urban kids, which means Black and Brown kids. And they're off the table, you know.

Marc: No doubt. Even the term "urban" has become a kind of secret-agent talk for race and class that allows us to talk about these issues, and these people, without having to name them or discuss them with honesty and purpose.

Mumia: Right! And when there is discussion about education, it's really threatening and beating down teachers, and framing teachers' unions as something anarchic and dangerous to the republic. In my lifetime, I've never seen teachers talked about so viciously as I have in the last four or five years. There used to be a time when, even though states and schools did not remunerate or pay them well, there was a residual of respect for the profession and respect for those people who served in the profession. I think that's all but gone.

Marc: Absolutely, man. The public discourse on education is definitely centered on anti-teacher rhetoric. So many of our public and private conversations on education begin with, *"If we could just get teachers to..."* That's deeply problematic. And these ideas are further reinforced through popular media. The most influential educational film of this new century has been *Waiting for Superman*, which is nothing more than thinly veiled anti-teacher, anti-union and anti-tenure propaganda. And this is nothing new. The film is merely the latest in a long string of films like *Stand and Deliver, To Sir With Love, Blackboard Jungle, Dangerous Minds, Dead Poets Society* or even *Summer School*. All these movies convey to the American people that the key to educational success is charismatic, and perhaps even messianic, leadership and a "get tough" approach. You don't need more books, you don't need more funding, you don't need to re-imagine the curriculum. All you need is teachers who "care" and a willingness to crack down on the teachers and parents who allegedly don't. And of course, you must always crack down on students.

Mumia: Right. There was also that movie out of New Jersey. I think the gentleman's name was Joseph Clark—

Marc: Yup, *Lean on Me!*

Mumia: Yeah, the dude with the baseball bat! I remember seeing that movie and being sickened by it. The depiction of the kids, and perhaps worse, the depiction of the parents! It was a naked attack on the Black community with the less than implicit message that what those niggas needed was to get beat down with a ball bat!

Marc: No doubt. That film, which my colleague Henry Giroux has written about with great depth and nuance, projects some very dangerous ideas about schooling.

Mumia: Well, in the film they essentially ejected all of the so-called "bad kids" out of the school, as if there was something useful to be learned in the streets. Teachers got kicked to the curb at the whim of a dictator. Arts programs, like the school choir's trip to Europe, got jettisoned. It was the glorification of the bullying of Black people by a tyrant. Of course, for their purposes, it was a Black tyrant.

Marc: Exactly. And it's no coincidence that Joe Clark was a registered Republican and was asked to be secretary of education in the Reagan Administration. Since then, he's become director of a youth detention center in New Jersey, where he was caught putting teenagers in shackles. His approach to education is entirely consistent with the neo-liberal and neo-conservative belief in market-based reform, high stakes testing, de-skilled teachers, authoritarian control and disposable youth.

Mumia: Exactly. And no one wants to talk about the resources that are extended to urban schools and how little they get because funding is determined by property taxes, and most people in inner cities are renters and therefore own little property or their properties aren't worth very much. So those who need the most get the least, and those who have the most get the most.

Marc: That's exactly right. And this economic arrangement is just a taken-for-granted part of American educational and social life.

Mumia: And the real tragedy is that America certainly has some of the best higher education in the world. People all over the world come here to attend colleges and universities. But how can you have such an extended, deep and rich higher educational system and such a pitiful primary and secondary educational system? It's bizarre to say the least.

Marc: Well, it's bizarre unless we think about the failing public education system as the impetus for installing new managerial logics. In other words, if we can convince the people that "public" is bad—not just public schools, but other public offerings like public housing or public options in health care—it becomes easier to usher in these new reform strategies that only serve the interests of the powerful and the privileged and the private. For example, the charter school movement, which has been celebrated by the so-called Educational Left as a pathway to new forms of democratic choice, does nothing but allow profiteers to chip away at public schools.

The charter school movement does nothing but allow profiteers to CHIP away at public schools.

Mumia: When I hear all this glorification of the charter schools, it makes me think of the continuing rebellion against *Brown*. I'll tell you why. If you listen to the voices of real, deep, right wing antipathy to public schools, they don't say "public schools," they say "government schools." As if the government has no role in educating its citizens, and as if this whole enterprise should be a private function. Charter schools reach perhaps six percent of the nation's kids—eff the hype! They certainly ain't no answer to the millions of kids—Black, Brown and White—who need and deserve a quality education!

Marc: Right. At their best, charter schools are laboratories of innovation whose insights can be brought back to traditional public schools for the good of everyone. In the current moment, however, they've become sites of economic exploitation and political opportunism. Corporate honchos are taking advantage of the New Markets Tax Credit, which gives federal tax breaks for new charter school construction. Once the buildings are built, they're rented out to public school districts at exorbitant rates. So, like prisons, charter schools become a cottage industry whose *raison d'être* is economic rather than educative. On top of that, the educational value of these institutions is grossly overstated. Of course, some charter schools do really well. And they should! After all, they put their thumbs on the scale. They have the ability to reject students with emotional and learning disabilities. They can kick students out with ease. Also, there's a "creaming effect," where the strongest students and most active parents are going to get their children out of struggling schools and send them to the shiny new charter school. Still, despite these advantages, only about 17 percent of charter schools outperform public schools, academically. The bigger issue is that, while they fetishize charter schools, many school reformists offer no solutions for the majority of students who are forced to remain in second-class schools.

Mumia: And this puts parents in a tough position because they want to do right by their kids and give them all the opportunities available. So many of them end up supporting charter schools.

Marc: That's because they feel like they have no other choice. They're unhappy with their current schools and charter schools at least give the illusion of choice, even if they're choosing between two equally undesirable options. As you said, parents want their kids to get high quality education.

Mumia: It's interesting that we didn't have this kind of discussion 40 or 50 years ago when public education seemed to at least serve the children of European immigrants far more than, say, Latino immigrants or Native Americans or Blacks. That whole dialogue has changed because this used to be seen as a system that lifted up people, that put them on the same fundamental level with everyone else by giving them the basics. This was a requirement, almost, for citizenship. Now, urban schools are precursors to prison. Marian Wright Edelman talks about these schools where they really inculcate prison culture in children so that they feel comfortable going from P.S. 103 into Rikers Island.

Marc: Right! Schools have very quickly become spaces that mirror broader post-9/11 society, with expanded surveillance and heightened militarization. When you walk into a school in North Philly or Watts or Harlem, there's a line 20 minutes long to get into the school. You have to pass by uniformed police officers, parole officers, drug sniffing dogs, hand scanners and metal detectors. And then, after taking 20 minutes to get into the school, you finally get in and look around and see that there ain't nobody stopping you from leaving!

Mumia: So that's to discourage your ass from gettin' in, but if you want to leave you can!

Marc: Exactly! That sends a certain kind of message, a kind of public pedagogy, about what matters to the school and the broader society. Like you said, it's all about containing and conditioning and disciplining bodies, preparing them for a prison-like existence. This is further facilitated by school discipline policies that criminalize our children for developmentally appropriate behavior. To borrow the language of Decoteau Irby, an expert on school discipline policy, schools have both widened and deepened the "discipline net." Schools have widened the net of disciplinary infractions, meaning that there's more stuff that you can get in trouble for in school. For example, bringing a pair of scissors to school is now a disciplinary violation when it wasn't, say, 20 years ago. But the net has also been deepened, so that there are greater penalties for the things that have always gotten you into trouble. As a result, yelling at a teacher no longer gets you a detention, but an arrest for disorderly conduct.

Mumia: When something like this happens, I think we're looking at the essence of neo-liberalism. In a cynical sense, we can see a form of education being performed, just a draconian and repressive form. I mean, with the flight of decent manufacturing jobs from the 'hood and the rise of the service economy, kids must be beaten down into accepting that their place in society is quite circumscribed. Dig me? So again, from the system's perspective, all signs of resistance must be extinguished. One must obey. I'm tempted to yell, like the dude in that movie: "This is Sparta!"

Marc: And these processes of discipline also function on other levels as well. You know, when I was going to school, they had this company called Channel One. They gave all the public schools free TVs and other equipment for every classroom. Of course, all the schools took them because they didn't have any money. The only commitment schools had to make was to have students spend the first 12 minutes of each school day watching their Channel One News report. Sounds like a good situation, right? But what happened is that we got about two minutes of news and 10 minutes of ads for pimple cream, TV shows, fashion and magazines. And, on top of that, the school's lunchroom had billboards for products and, of course, the armed forces. Pizza Hut sponsored our reading program. Our bodies and minds were being trained, disciplined really, for the military, for the consumer market, for everything except democratic citizenship.

Mumia: But in a certain sense, we have to ask, "When have Blacks really, truly, been citizens?" The closest that we've come to being citizens has been when Black men and women served in the armies of the empire. And I don't want to sound facetious, but if we can't walk down the street, drive, go into a store...

Marc: ...then we ain't citizens.

Mumia: We're told we're citizens, and we're taught in school about being citizens, but when does that thing become real? In public schools, where kids get punished for thinking? In schools which do more to kill the mind than to teach or expand it? We are citizens, I think, in the same sense that the old Huns were "citizens" of Rome. They served Rome; Rome didn't serve them. And when I read Roman history, I'm struck by how alienated they were from Roman society. In a real sense, we are in this society, but not of it.

Marc: Right now, schools are so committed to containment, punishment, and narrow ideas of success that we squander their true potential. You can't get the rich environment, you can't inherit deep intellectual traditions and you can't even gain the requisite knowledge to thrive in those esteemed higher educational institutions. Too many of our children are merely trained to become cogs in a machine, to become alienated workers, to become beings acted upon rather than actively functioning as agents in the world.

Mumia: In some ways, it's worse than that because this is America, where schools have been the doorway to class betterment. And when you create schools as an obstacle course—where people are beaten down psychologically, intellectually, and emotionally—you close the doors and the gates to the whole society. And that's dysfunction.

Marc: So if we start from the place that the educational system is indeed dysfunctional, and we acknowledge how high the stakes are with regard to education and social prosperity, how should we think about reimagining education for Black people?

Mumia: Well, I think that's a good question and a good starting place. But I don't think the answer is as radical as the question suggests. Education has been—and I'm talking strictly in American terms—a democratizing institution in American life that has worked quite well for White people. It took them off the farm, you dig what I'm saying? It gave them essentially an urbanized education. And for those people who came back from World War II, they now had access to higher education because of the GI Bill. So it worked for them excellently. Why is it now difficult to work for black people who were former peasants, who more than any other people in America are truly hungry for education?

Marc: No doubt. The GI Bill was the seedbed that literally produced the White American middle class. As always, those opportunities were never properly distributed to Black folk. And to that end, I think the answer to solving our educational problems is actually very radical. We have to start from the place of saying that schools as they currently function simply don't work. And then we have to begin to develop an entirely new way of thinking about how to engage our children within the educational system. Given everything we know about our history in America, there's no reason to think that this is going to change on its own.

Mumia: And it seems to me that education is difficult when it comes to Black children in ways that it isn't when it comes to White children. And you see that when you study Lisa Delpit's *Other People's Children* or the work of Jonathan Kozol, who has probably written more than anyone in this country on education. Black children go through schools and get beaten psychologically and emotionally by teachers and disciplinarians.

Marc: And I would argue that the majority of the teachers who educate our children don't suffer from a lack of desire or willingness to teach their students well. I think most teachers want to be effective, but are hamstrung by pre-figured scripted curricula that essentially de-skill them, reducing them to assembly-line workers. The nation's obsession with testing, which

Black children go through schools and get BEATEN psychologically and emotionally by teachers and disciplinarians.

has only intensified through policies like No Child Left Behind, has undermined teachers' ability to reach students in interesting, innovative and culturally responsive ways. On top of that, many teachers are culturally disconnected from Black students. After all, 90 percent of the nation's teaching force, and 70 percent of the nation's urban teaching force, is White. I'm not saying that White teachers can't teach Black students, or that Black teachers always get it right, but the race gap does present another structural obstacle.

Mumia: I think you've touched on something very vital here, man. Imagine you are a young White woman, who has just earned her degree in education. And as a new, raw hire, you're put into a Black, actually segregated, primary school environment? What do you do? First, you are rarely able to really communicate with the kids who come from profoundly different cultural communities than you. That's why I keep referencing Lisa Delpit's writing, because it illustrates how some teachers interact with children from a presumption that their language is not just different, but wrong, silly and stupid—something to be ashamed of. Delpit actually gained her insights while traveling and teaching in Papua, New Guinea. Teachers teach far more than the curriculum in class. They teach "place," meaning an understanding of where a kid stands in relation to society. If teachers were trained to really hear and respect Ebonics, they'd be able to appreciate its rhythms, its intonations and histories locked within it. Then they could teach kids new ways of language. Otherwise, school is just another place where we're told to sit down, shut up and obey.

Marc: Unfortunately, that is too often what schools have become. And these disconnects have real consequences. For example, Black students, especially boys, are overrepresented in special education classes. Often times, they're placed in special education because of behavioral, rather than intellectual, issues. And on the behavioral side, our children make up 17 percent of the nation's school population, but constitute 36 percent of out-of-school suspensions and 32 percent of expulsions. The thing is, though, we're not getting suspended for clear and objective violations of school discipline policies, like bringing guns and drugs to school or punching someone in the face. The bulk of our children's suspensions and expulsions come from what researcher Russell Skiba calls "disciplinary moments," where teachers have to make *subjective* interpretations of our children's behavior. In other words, they have to decide whether or not our children are being "disrespectful" or "too loud" or "threatening." Given the troublesome social and cultural scripts that the world has about Black children—that they're dangerous, violent, unintelligent, immoral and lazy—it's difficult for even well-meaning teachers to get it right without serious work. For us to address the current educational crisis, we must start taking these issues seriously. Oftentimes, however, this is difficult because of the faith that our people have in the promise of education.

Mumia: That faith is very deep, bro. I mean, my father and my mother used to tell me, "The only thing the White man can't take from you is that edumacation." I mean, if I heard it five times, I heard it 1,100 times! I think they remembered from the tales of their elders when reading and writing was a killing offense. But I also think they recalled when folks who didn't know how to read or count could be, and were, cheated out of some things. I bet you that 90 percent of all the folks who traveled North did so because they wanted to give their kids a better education!

Marc: That's because Black people in America, even as slaves, have always imagined education as a direct pathway to citizenship: *If we can* *just read, if we can just get these books, if we can just learn this Bible, if we can just sign our name on these contracts, then we will be fuller citizens. We can get everything that democracy has to offer.* And on some level it was true. I mean, when Frederick Douglass learns to read he is liberated, right?

Mumia: True.

Marc: But it seems like now we're invested in education in a very different, maybe even less authentic, way.

Mumia: Well, I think you're right, but the reasons are really twofold. We've changed and the nation has changed. But again, what we cannot ignore are the systematic obstructions that Black people met when going into these fundamentally alien institutions and systems. We went in with the best of objectives and purposes but we met roadblocks. Malcolm X is perhaps the best known because he talked to his teacher and said, *"I want to be a lawyer"* and the teacher basically said, *"Come on nigga, be realistic."*

Marc: Right. A lot of us have had that experience!

Mumia: And of course, Malcolm was one of the most brilliant… I don't want to say "self-taught" because he was really taught by the Nation of Islam, and taught well. But he became a brilliant orator, a great writer and a hell of an organizer.

Marc: That's a great point. When I think about Malcolm or read your book *Jailhouse Lawyers*, it seems to me that much of the education that Black folk get is from other institutions and spaces. In other words, we've always made a critical distinction between education and schooling. This is how Malcolm could get rejected by a teacher and have his aspirations cooled down. But then, later in life, he had those aspirations heated up through the Nation of Islam. He pulls out that dictionary and begins to read, but then the Nation of Islam gives him something to read for. The Nation gives him something to fight for. It makes education relevant to his lived reality again. Our churches have also done that. The Black Panther Party did that. These institutions and organizations gave us something tangible. They gave us an education that was unavailable through formal schooling. We certainly still see that phenomenon in the prisons. I mean, you see brothers finding education in prison all the time, right?

Mumia: Well they get it, but they get it informally from other brothers. It's not very different from Malcolm's experience. They get it from other brothers, elders, or if they're lucky enough and have some resources, they can do something through the mail. But in terms of formal education offered by the institution, that's a rare thing because of cost. But also I think because of interest. You might be able to get a GED and you might be able to get some college courses, but you gotta have ends. Remember, one of the things that Clinton did is extinguish Pell Grants for prisoners. He wiped out a whole cohort of guys who would deeply benefit from a decent education, and gave them nothing to fill the gap. And it's really pitiful when you consider that people who study these joints, so-called criminologists will tell you that the only thing that works in terms of defeating recidivism is education.

Marc: Right. Yet we systematically eliminate the very thing that can stop the crisis of incarceration, which only reinforces the idea that the school-to-prison pipeline is a very deliberate and well-planned reality. We don't want people to get an education because then we wouldn't be able to keep feeding Black bodies to the prison industry.

Mumia: Right!

Marc: This says to me that Black people need to intervene. One of the great disappointments that I have with Black folk has been that we've completely surrendered our children to these systems. Of course, we need to demand from the government all that it owes us. Because we are *citizens*. At the same time, we have to know that the government is never going to give us the tools for our liberation. That means that we need our own schools, our own institutions, our own communities where we give our children the type of education that they need for freedom. And I'm wondering where we can find examples of that.

Mumia: Well, we used to be able to find it widespread in the '60s. We find it very rarely today and I think it's because of the class divide in Black America. Because the institutions that have the resources are now disconnected from working class African-Americans and poor people who populate the prisons. But you made an interesting statement when you talked about education and schooling that really rang in my mind. It reminded me of an old quote from Mark Twain, who said, " I never let my schooling interfere with my education."

The government is NEVER going to give us the tools for our liberation.

Marc: Exactly! And that's what I'm saying, man. We have to make that distinction. I'm now thinking of my own informal learning experiences growing up. The things that have mattered the most and affected me the most, and even driven me to get more formal schooling, were things I learned outside of school. It was the books I read outside of school. It was the community bookstores like Hakim's on 52nd Street in Philadelphia. It was everything outside of school that made me think that knowledge wasn't just an instrumental thing, where I would get diplomas and credentials just to get a job or be able to read well enough to put together a bookshelf or order from a menu. I came to believe that information could actually change my life in valuable ways. This was a relatively radical idea that had nothing to do with my school experiences.

Mumia: Think again of your example of Frederick Douglass. He knew exactly what his "massah" meant when he said, *"If you let that boy learn how to read you'll spoil a nigga."* And Douglass was like, *"Oh is that it? I've got to find this out!"*

Marc: Right. "If they don't want me to have it then it must be something good with it." And part of what Douglass modeled is this idea of radical literacy, of radical education. I'm talking about the idea that Black folk can use these bodies of knowledge in the service of justice and freedom if we make that critical distinction between education and schooling. Schooling ain't helping us very much right now.

Mumia: With the exception of perhaps Dr. Martin Luther King, why is it that most profound thinkers and activists and leaders in the 20th century were men who were formally uneducated? The Honorable Elijah Muhammad went through third grade; Malcolm essentially dropped out of high school and got educated in the prison cell; Huey P. Newton went back to school to earn his doctorate later but initially they called him illiterate.

Marc: Yet each of them located other spaces for necessary forms of education. The Honorable Elijah Muhammad was trained by Master Fard Muhammad, who encouraged him to read 104 books. He also studied with the Moorish Science Temple and other organizations that provided him with crucial bodies of knowledge about his racial history and identity. Much of this information became the foundation for Malcolm X, who read even further and wider, from literature to political theory. By the time Huey was studying for his Ph.D. at UC Santa Cruz, he'd already mastered the nuances of Marxist theory in ways that rivaled credentialed scholars. Even Martin Luther King gained critical information not only from Morehouse and Boston University, but from activists, organizers and everyday people. We have to find a way to take the best of these traditions and approaches and link them to the educational experiences of our children. You shouldn't have to go to prison or join a revolution to get a quality and liberatory education.

Mumia: Well, you *shouldn't* but…

Marc: That's just how it be sometimes!

Mumia: No doubt! But on the serious side, prison *was* school for Malcolm X. That was his university. And for thousands of ANC militants in South Africa, prisons were Mandela Universities! But you're right that it shouldn't be that way. And that's where that citizenship thing comes into play. Too many of us, especially those involved in national and communal organizations, have left the field of this very serious social challenge. We have failed to perform the task of educating the young. Perhaps it's time for the old

Freedom Schools to re-emerge, perhaps sponsored by a collaboration of prominent rappers. Perhaps every social- or activist-type group should be charged with doing it for, say, 500 or 5,000 kids in their office's immediate vicinity. Where are the churches, which were once the center of our struggle to gain literacy? I think this thing is so serious that we all have a hand in it. And we must address, and indeed erase, the class divide. Most of our middle-class brothers and sisters are a hair's breadth away from returning to the ghetto. If we don't beat this, then our future is tarnished indeed.

Marc: Yes, and the consequences aren't just economic. Our very lives are at stake.

Mumia: For sure. My wife told me several years ago that she went to pick up our grandson at school. The recess was being called over and the teacher yelled, "Yaaaard Uppp! Yaaard Upppp!" That's what they say in prison. Now that's ugly.

It's time for the freedom schools of the '60s to RE-EMERGE, perhaps sponsored by a collaboration of prominent rappers.

Marc: That's ugly and *scary*. And unless we take it upon ourselves to re-imagine and change our approach to education and schooling, that's our collective destiny.

FOR YOUR LIBRARY

Education of Blacks in the South, 1860-1935, **James D. Anderson**

Educating The "Right" Way, **Michael W. Apple**

Schooling in Capitalist America, **Samuel Bowles and Herbert Gintis**

Other People's Children, **Lisa Delpit**

Democracy and Education, **John Dewey**

Bad Boys, **Ann Ferguson**

Theory and Resistance in Education **and** *Stealing Innocence*,
Henry A. Giroux

Beats, Rhymes, and Classroom Life, **Marc Lamont Hill**

The Shame of the Nation **and** *Savage Inequalities*,
Jonathan Kozol

Forgotten Readers, **Elizabeth McHenry**

The Death and Life of the Great American School System,
Diane Ravitch

Education as Enforcement, **Kenneth J. Saltman**
and David A. Gabbard, eds.

The Mis-Education of the Negro, **Carter G. Woodson**

CHAPTER 7

Black Love

In this conversation, we discuss the role of love across every dimension of Black life. Although we were excited by this opportunity—in this culture, there are few safe spaces for Black men to talk about love, especially with each other—we were scared of the personal layers that we would inevitably uncover as we dug deeper into the conversation. Fortunately, we ran toward our fears and engaged in a difficult but necessary dialogue about the critical role that love has played throughout every period of Black life. The conversation also forced us to confront, in many cases for the first time, some of our most personal and painful issues with love and relationships. In doing so, we hope to model the type of open, honest and reflective dialogues that are necessary for learning, growing and healing.

Marc: When we decided to have these conversations, we were both excited about the idea of including love as one of the topics. I must admit, though, it's been the most difficult one for me to think about. I wasn't quite sure how to frame it or where to begin.

Mumia: Well, when I thought about it, my real feeling was, *How do we express it? How do Black people express love in the United States of America?* It's ironic that the people who are the most despised, the most unloved in American history, have essentially been the avatars of love.

Marc: That's so true.

Mumia: It even plays out in our music. Millions of people are alive today because of some Black musician. Johnny Mathis, Dionne Warwick, Aretha, Tina Turner, Ron Isley, Sade, Toni Braxton, Whitney Houston...

Marc: You can't forget Luther, man! You can't forget Luther!

Mumia: Right. You can't forget Loofa—Big Loofa or Little Loofa! All of them sang love songs that turned people on. And not just Black folks—all folks. They made magic with their music. They made love music. That's Black love.

Marc: It is, man. And it seems like so much of what Black people have collectively done in America has been animated by love. Whether it's our music tradition, the art or our political struggles, in our best moments we've always been driven by love. But it seems to me that the conversation about love, in whatever form, isn't happening in the same

The conversation we're having about LOVE isn't happening in the same way it used to.

way. The music doesn't talk about love as much. When you look at our political struggles, and what we do on the ground as activists, the love piece seems to be missing. I can't help but think of bell hooks, whose writings on love have been my biggest influence and inspiration. She once pointed out that at the Million Man March, there was not one prominent speaker who spoke about love as a primary talking point or organizing principle.

Mumia: That's a very astute observation. Very insightful. And it's true. I think of a non-Black person, Che Guevara, who said, "True revolutionaries are guided by great feelings of love." That is perhaps his best known and most powerful axiom. And I think it's the truth.

Marc: Yes! That's what made bell hooks's observation so powerful to me. For Black people to organize politically without love at the center is to ignore the very thing that has sustained us here in America. We've always fought back, we've always resisted, we've always challenged the status quo. All of this is an outgrowth of our will not only to survive, but to love.

Mumia: Yes. Look at the people who animate our spirits, whether it's Ella Baker, Angela Y. Davis, Martin or Malcolm, The Honorable Elijah Muhammad, Du Bois or Douglass. All these folks, to do what they did took tremendous courage, but also tremendous love of Black folks.

Marc: Yeah. The idea that people are willing to risk their very lives reflects a profound love of Black people. We talked about the ethic of risk when we spoke about leadership, the idea that you are willing to risk your own body, livelihood and future to produce a world that you won't even see. The idea of people risking their lives for a world that their children or children's children would enjoy. This requires a different kind of love than many of us can appreciate at the current moment. So when I think about this young 21st century, I can't help but worry that there's a profound lack of love. I'm not saying that Black people don't love each other anymore. That kind of thinking is too simplistic and reactionary. But certainly, love is not at the center of the conversation. And to me that is very disturbing.

Mumia: Marc, I think it's even more than you say. The Martins and the Malcolms were, of course, messianic figures. They knew they would not live in the Promised Land. But remember, they did it not for their grand-children, but for the hope that their grandchildren would inhabit a different world.

Marc: Yes! That hope piece is crucial. Otherwise love becomes too simple, too calculated. Love, of any sort, requires an emotional risk. If not, love would be easy. It requires us to put our hearts and spirits in the hands of others, to put our very selves on the line. Love requires that we offer

Love requires that we offer ourselves without worries of RECIPROCITY or mutuality.

ourselves without worries of reciprocity or mutuality. It demands that we submerge our egos. Love doesn't ignore fear, hate and indifference, nor does it deny the material conditions and challenges that we face. It simply refuses to be prisoner to them. Love is revolutionary.

Mumia: Absolutely. For everyone, but especially for Black people, love is the most revolutionary force there is. From the very beginning of our time here in America, since 1619, the forces put into place structures that projected hatred of Black life. They literally criminalized Black love. That stuff still echoes down the centuries; laws written before there was a United States still bounce around in our heads. It's crazy. I mean, marriage was illegal! We were forced to hurt each other, rewarded for it. That's got to have echoes in our consciousness.

Marc: One of the ironies of American life is that Black folk, at all moments, have offered the most profound examples of love at the very same time that the notion of Black love has been rendered oxymoronic. I mean, the idea that we're full human beings is new to many folk. Shit, for some it's still a futuristic idea!

Mumia: For sure!

Marc: The idea that we have the capacity to love, to care and to have regard for one another is still being called into question. And yet at every moment, Blacks have attempted to love our way through the absurdity of our experience here in America. Slaves, for God's sake, were beaten and abused yet they were still praying for relief not only for themselves but for their cruel slave masters. Black folk were getting hit with batons and water hoses for the purpose of Black freedom, but also for trying to love White people into a new sense of humanity. We've always been the barometers. We've always been the conscience. We've always been the index of America's love ethic. That, to me, is a remarkable testimony to our people and to the transformative power of love.

Mumia: That's right. And I think that's why we've always had this cultural space that I mentioned earlier. And it's a sad thing that many members of this generation have gone into adulthood without expressing that love, even romantic love. Because romantic love ain't "cool," you know what I mean? Think about Tupac, whose biggest hit for many people was "Dear Mama." It was about love for his mama. Now most dudes would say that ain't cool. But guess what? When they heard it, they felt it. They didn't express it verbally, but I bet a whole lot of dudes went into their room and cried. They didn't want their homies to see them tears. Or think about Tupac's other song "Brenda's Got A Baby." That's about love, man! That's about a profound love for a young sister. And he's screaming about her essence, her worth, just like he was screaming about his mama: "Even as a crack fiend, mama. You always was a Black queen, mama." That's strong.

Marc: Exactly. And I think Black love is complex like that. Even when you read Toni Morrison's *Beloved*, where Sethe makes the decision to kill her baby rather than allowing her to be born into slavery, you can see how complex it is. Black love has never been purely romantic, and it damn sure ain't been easy. It has often involved levels of sacrifice, dislocation, abandonment and pain. But at the end of the day, there's always been a fundamental regard for another person's existence that is so deep that it drives us to ends that we otherwise couldn't have reached, even for ourselves. And that to me is the beautiful thing about Black love.

Mumia: For no other people in America has love been criminalized. Not even "the wild savage Indians." They were "noble savages," or at least projected as such. But love was a crime for Black people. You couldn't marry the woman of your heart. And you certainly couldn't protect the children of your loins and of your spirit. You couldn't protect your mother or father. Love was illegal. Sex was illicit, but love was illegal because we were not supposed to be people. If we loved, then we would be understood as people instead of the chattel that the law called us.

Marc: Right. So Black love becomes this thing that's always...

Mumia: Subversive.

Marc: Yes! I'm reminded of Assata Shakur's poem, where she says, "Love is contraband in hell."

Mumia: There you go.

Marc: Of course, Assata was talking about her relationship with Kamau

Sadiki. While they were standing trial together for a trumped up charge, they conceived a child. Despite being locked inside the dungeons of prison, where the body and mind are supposed to be controlled by the State, they were able to produce a beautiful daughter. Their love was a revolutionary act, a powerful act of resistance to State repression and violence. As she put it, "We are pregnant with love. We are a conspiracy."

Mumia: Beautiful.

Marc: But on a broader level, Assata is speaking to Black people's existence in America, and really around the globe. As you often say, we're living in hell. And so our love becomes a kind of contraband for which we are constantly punished.

Mumia: And yet we continue to love.

Marc: Yes, we do. And to me, that's all we can do. A commitment to loving ourselves through the madness of this world is our only weapon. For me, that love takes many forms: loving our children, loving our partners, loving our community and loving freedom enough to stand up and fight for it. I'm not talking about love as empty sentimentality or gutless passivity. I'm talking about something active, deliberate, and courageous. To borrow from Ntozake Shange, we have to love each other on purpose.

Mumia: I hear you, but loving *ourselves* is still such a struggle. If others around us project onto us that we're unlovable, then some of us are not only going to feel it but also believe it. I'm reminded of an interview I saw years ago with bell hooks. She described a conversation she had with Lil' Kim. She got around to asking Kim about love and Kim responded with something like, *"What is that? I don't know what love is."* Her comment actually reminded me of Tina Turner's blockbuster hit, "What's Love Got To Do With It?" Now what makes this particularly poignant is the fact that the interview was done before her blonde ambition phase.

Marc: Right. And with Lil' Kim, even before she became a celebrity, she had a fundamental sense of alienation from the very idea of love. Although I don't know Kim, I'm convinced that there's a relationship between her feelings of lovelessness and the kind of self-mutilation that she's engaged in over the past decade through various forms of plastic surgery.

Mumia: It's a shame, man. Before her transfiguration, with her natural nose and dark hair, Lil' Kim was a sho' nuff beauty if you ask me!

Marc: I agree. That's why your point about self-love is so critical. In the context of White supremacy, it is so difficult for Black folk to fully love ourselves. The world constantly tells us that we have the wrong faces, the wrong body parts, the wrong culture and the wrong values. While most Black folks don't have the resources to do the kinds of things that Kim did, many of us have the same impulse. How do we respond to this?

Mumia: Well if we don't love ourselves, no one will. And love, being energy, radiates through us into the outer world—into the universe beyond. I don't think our people were more powerful than when we fought for our freedom. Not out of fear, but out of love. That love charged and changed the way the world looked at us and responded to us. So we gotta dig how powerful our vibration can be.

Marc: Word. There's so much public conversation in the last year or two about Black love and more specifically Black relationships. Countless television specials, best-selling books and magazine articles have all been dedicated to the topic. How do you see them in the 21st century?

Mumia: Well we can't divorce Black love and Black relationships from the material realities that every person, but specifically every Black man, faces in this culture. And the reality of the situation is that White men are threatened by Black men.

Marc: In what ways?

Mumia: I think because they see them as competitors to the material goodies and wealth that this society possesses. After all, in capitalist thinking, property is not just the highest good, but the essence of societal power, the germ of worth. In this country, we may not worship kings and princes, but we worship wealth because wealth is shorthand for power. Like Lil' Kim and the Lox said "First you get the money, then you get the power, then you get respect!" As a result, we run up against this eternal wall. White men are less threatened, and in some cases not threatened, by Black women. So Black women get a kind of access that Black men have not yet received. This happens in business and education for sure, but really in all major fields of American life. I don't think it's a coincidence that the most prominent Black figure in entertainment, Oprah Winfrey, is a Black woman. I think that's structural in a way.

Marc: That's interesting and it's certainly an argument that I hear a lot. Brothers often say, "They put women in universities and put us in prisons." You really think that's true?

Mumia: I think it's true, at least psychologically. My generation grew up in this society watching Roy Rogers. You know, those cowboy shows where the good guy was the White cowboy and the bad guy was the Indian. We saw that as kids and believed it! We wanted to be cowboys when we grew up! You know what I mean? So we have the same kind of fictions and myths in our head. And so a guy wants to be able to do what? Not just love and marry and bring children forth but to support his family. And if the social structure is such that women are able to get the material goodies far easier and at a higher rate than men, then in many cases there's a real imbalance in that relationship. Because many women grow up with the idea that a man is supposed to take care of the family, they'll cut a dude loose when he doesn't have the kind of income that she likes. Remember one of the biggest hits of the '90s was "No Scrubs": *If you live at home wit' ya mama…*" So that's very real. And while it should not affect the affairs of the heart, this is America.

Marc: That's real. So in some sense, a patriarchal and heteronormative vision of the family governs those types of relationships. I know some people would argue that relationships governed by male dominance—you know, men bringing home the bacon and the women frying it—can never really be filled with love. But I just can't believe that, given the deep history we've had in this country with grandmama and grandpapa, and great-grandmama and great-grandpapa living under those circumstances but certainly loving each other deeply. At the same time, I believe that we must challenge this ideology if we are going to love each other more fully. After all, underneath those material conditions you mentioned is still a patriarchal vision that says men are supposed to be taking care of women, and that women are supposed to be taking care of homes and children. I think that dismantling that patriarchal framework is the only way that we can have a shot at healthy and more thoroughly loving relationships, you know?

Mumia: You know what, Marc? Given how some of us were raised, and certainly in not-too-distant Black history, the truth of the matter is that most of us didn't grow up in those kinds of patriarchal families. Mom was working outside the home. And I know from reading feminist literature that millions of Black women, in the South and up North, worked in White homes, either in domestic work or as nurses, working to support their families. So, all too often, patriarchal imagery is one imposed by outer culture, through TV or other projection devices, into homes and heads that didn't see that in their everyday lived lives. And again, that too was a material reality in that so few Black men were making living wages that Black women had to work. Also, because they were dehumanized, White society saw nothing wrong with Black women doing work. After all, they weren't White women.

Marc: I don't know about that, Mu. It was economic pressure, not an anti-patriarchal ideology that forced Black women out of the house. The White community's willingness to allow Black women into the workplace also allowed them to keep White women on the domestic pedestal, reifying the differences between Black and White women in terms of their fundamental "womanhood" and, by extension, their fundamental humanity. At the same time it was a shot against Black men, as White men could now say, *"Our women are home like a woman is supposed to be while yours are in our houses, fields and factories working."* But all of this only makes sense within a patriarchal framework, a world in which male humanity is measured by the extent to which we can control the destinies of Black women. And even if we push aside the labor piece, our homes have always been filled with other forms of patriarchy with regard to child rearing, domestic labor and sex. We're still trying to shake some of that stuff off. But much of it we've just come to romantically and uncritically accept as "conservative" or "old school" values.

The pain of fatherlessness, of early rejection and abandonment, has produced an entire generation of brothers and sisters who are deeply WOUNDED.

Mumia: I hear you. That's an important point you're making.

Marc: At the same time, I think you're right to point out that we have had other models for family life and relationships than the ones we look to now. History is certainly instructive in that regard. I just want to be careful about not overstating how progressive we've been. Now, another material reality that we have to confront is the fracture of our families. Over the last few decades, we've seen a mass exodus of fathers from our homes, due at least in part to the decline of the urban economy and the rise of the prison industrial complex. How does that impact how we understand and negotiate love?

Mumia: We suffered real serious danger during the '80s and '90s during the Crack Era. The poet Marvin X writes about it better than anyone I've ever read. Also, you sent me a copy of Jay-Z and dream hampton's excellent book *Decoded*. Jay-Z makes the point about how deeply he was wounded when his old man split. He also said something like, *"We had to create our own fathers and our own ancestors. We found 'em on wax."* I said, "Damn!"

Marc: Yes. The pain of fatherlessness, of early rejection and abandonment, has produced an entire generation of brothers and sisters who are deeply wounded. In some ways, we've become wounded healers. After all, as Jay-Z points out in *Decoded*, the hip-hop generation has turned the absentee father into a social pariah within our community. Hip-hop has made it thoroughly uncool to abandon your kids. We've forced the next generation to live up to a different standard of responsibility and love. At the same time, we're still carrying these wounds that affect how we navigate the world. On his song "December 4th," Jay-Z says: "The teachers couldn't reach me / and my mama couldn't beat me / hard enough to match the pain of my pop not seeing me / so, with that disdain in my membrane / got on my pimp game / 'fuck the world' my defense came." He's speaking to the lifelong trauma that this kind of stuff causes and how it undermines our ability to navigate the world in healthy and functional ways. Until we figure out how to address those wounds, we'll continue to struggle with love in every aspect of our lives.

Mumia: If love, in its broadest sense, is at the heart of our struggles, it'll bear the psychological fruit of healthier, more fully formed human beings. I remember back in the Black Panther Party when sisters got pregnant, which was often, they were essentially dispatched home—away from the "real work" of the organization. In hindsight, that was the dumbest thing in the world, for what "work" could be more important than motherhood? What could be more important than raising and teaching the next generation? A lot of us had pretty narrow ideas. If the Black Panther Party had built homes for sisters who became moms, made room for them, the Party might still be in existence today.

Marc: I agree. Obviously, I wasn't there in the '60s and '70s, but I can't imagine an organization functioning for any length of time if it doesn't keep women and children at its center. Now I'm sure that brothers thought that they were doing the right thing by keeping pregnant women away from the day-to-day activity of the Party, but I agree with you that it's a mistake on multiple levels. So who or what do we look to for proper models of love and relationships? It seems that everything we've discussed is so flawed and fractured.

Mumia: When we look back in history deep enough and far enough, we'll always find a lot of models that are helpful to our present. When our people emerged from bondage, I don't think there was anyone in America who rushed so quickly to get two things: an education and a marriage certificate. There are people who treasure the marriage papers of their grandparents or great-grandparents. They may not be able to find the freedom papers but they can find the marriage papers. Those *were* our freedom papers.

Marc: And I think a lot of the talk these days is still around marriage, right? But without all the substantive stuff underneath it. People always talk about the number of babies born "out of wedlock," the large number of Black women who are "never married," and the huge number of Black men who are "not marriageable" because of incarceration, joblessness and other issues. But it seems to me that marriage almost becomes an empty symbol—or a mere proxy for economic and social privilege. But we're talking not just about a decline in marriage, but a decline in healthy and functional relationships, relationships that are undergirded by love and care and respect.

Mumia: Well, we either learn from history or we stumble on down a dark street with mud in our eyes. In traditional African societies, people didn't marry one-to-one, but into clans, communities and collective bodies. That's because they understood that one who marries has impact far beyond that individual. So a great deal of thought was devoted to this practice. But in the West, let's be honest man, it's a contract. Indeed, in law, it is a contractual relationship. And up until recently, the woman's personhood became subsumed within a man's.

Marc: Exactly. Many intellectuals, both economists and feminist scholars, have even argued that marriage is merely legalized prostitution, a gendered exchange of goods and services authorized by the State.

Mumia: But surely we can do better than this! I often wonder about the sister, Black Eve, back at the dawn of humanity, giving that first Black birth, giving birth to all humankind. She transmitted something powerful and resilient: love. Without that, what stopped her from hurling that caterwauling beast away from her? And from that first primal relationship came all of us, all of this! You mean to tell me that after all this time, we can't love? We can't care? We can't transmit that love? We can't create forms that enrich us all in loving, life-affirming wholeness? I can't believe that. I refuse to believe that.

Marc: Me too. I think we both are making a critical distinction between marriage as life commitment and marriage as statecraft, even though I suspect that you ascribe more value to the former than I do.

Mumia: You're probably right.

Marc: Still, I don't disagree that Black people have the capacity and a need to produce loving relationships. I also don't deny the value, both individually and collectively, of affirming our bonds through formal commitments. But we also have to figure out the stuff from traditional family models, both American and African, that hasn't worked. I'm not anti-marriage at all, but I don't want us to fetishize marriage, either. Otherwise, we end up buying into this conservative idea that poor Black people can marry their way out of poverty, unemployment or other forms of social death. I also don't want us to be romantic about the traditional family model. After all, man, I grew up in a two-parent household, but there were many things that happened—or didn't happen—that have made it more difficult for me to engage in healthy and functional relationships. I'm still struggling to unlearn a life's worth of lessons just so that I can be whole, just so that I can be capable of loving someone fully. How about you? What was it like for you growing up? What types of relationships did you have access to? How did they affect your own ability to function in relationships?

Mumia: My parents were two country people trying to make it happen. Not legally, but where it matters: in the heart. My old man was born in 1897—

Marc: —Word? My pop was born in 1928, but damn, 1897?

Mumia: Yep. He was an old man for real! And while he and moms had their ups and downs, they loved each other and treated each other that way. But when I looked at other dude's pops, you know what I noticed about mine?
Marc: What's that?

Mumia: He spoke softly and very seldom. He was gentle. And he kissed his children incessantly. When I looked around at other dudes, they

My parents, were products of their time and didn't hug much or discuss their feelings. As a result, I swallowed what I felt and became emotionally UNAVAILABLE in relationships.

might get punched in the mouth by their old man, but I never saw a pop kiss his kid! I don't remember seeing that. As for mom, she was a soft-spoken country gal. Smart. Perceptive. But when I think of where she expressed her love overtly, like most sisters of her era, it was in church. Sisters tolerated your dumb ass, but they *loved* them some Jesus. I think what that did was make me, in some ways, emotionally distant. And like her, I spent a lot of time in religious structures, looking for things that weren't there.

Marc: My parents provided for each other, raised three boys together and built a life that their parents could only dream of. They were always willing to fight for us and tried to fulfill all of our needs and many of our wants. There was never any doubt that they loved us deeply. At the same time, like your parents, they were products of their time who demonstrated their love in very particular ways. They weren't huggers or kiss-ers, not of their children or each other. We didn't talk very much about our feelings except when we were conveying anger. This was particularly difficult for me because I was a very sensitive child. I was very in tune with my emotions. I had to learn to swallow many of my feelings of hurt and loneliness, insecurity and vulnerability. I had to hide much of my pain. As a result, like you, I became alienated from my feelings and grew colder and more emotionally distant. I was physically present but emotionally unavailable in most of my relationships. I grew up craving affection and attention at the same time that I was often incapable of providing those very things to the people in my life. I'm committed to changing that pattern. I'm committed to healing. But it's hard as hell. I ain't nowhere close to "there" yet.

Mumia: It sure is, bro. But we can't erase our history. Changing and healing is all we can do.

Marc: Exactly. That's why I get frustrated with books like Steve Harvey's *Act Like a Lady, Think Like a Man*, which still forces us to operate from an adversarial place. Such an approach prepares us to "win" rather than to heal, to view each other as means rather than ends. Also, by advancing the idea that dishonesty, hypersexuality and unreliability are "just the way men are," we normalize what is truly a sociopathic set of behaviors. To me, that's a really scary and dangerous way to think about relationships.

Mumia: Well it comes from the capitalist culture that we're in. We're influenced and colored by these material relations that affect how we move in this society, things like where we live, where our children go to school and what and how we eat. It also impacts our love relationships because there are a whole lot of brothers that are off the list.

Marc: What do you mean by "off the list"? You mean in terms of not being desirable to women because of their circumstance?

Mumia: I mean that they don't even merit "possibility" status because of past criminal convictions, educational deficits or our manner of moving in the world. In many meaningful ways, they are AWL: Absent With Leave. In terms of positive social interaction, we are nonentities. And if they're off one list then they're going to find another because that drive is so strong.

Marc: So do we still love sisters, Mu? I mean, on a fundamental level, do Black men love Black women?

Mumia: I think we have a profound and abiding love for Black women. But the fact of the matter is that it's *some* Black women and *some* times. And to be perfectly honest, it's a love/hate thing. We say we love them and we dream about them lovingly, but we don't treat 'em like we love 'em.

Marc: Right! It's like we love the *idea* of loving Black women but on a real fundamental level, I'm not so sure we do. Consider the R. Kelly controversy. R. Kelly is not like the O.J. Simpson case, where people actually dispute whether or not he did it. I don't know anybody who doesn't think that it was R. Kelly on the videotape having sex with underage girls.

Mumia: Right.

Marc: But even after being caught, R. Kelly ends up with a Number One album, *The Chocolate Factory*, with the megahit "Step in the Name of Love." Since then, he's remained popular and commercially successful, making hits with and for other hip-hop and R&B stars. Of course, there's the race piece. After all, if R. Kelly had been caught on tape with White girls, he'd be in prison. But let's also consider what would happen if it had been Black *boys* on the tape. Wouldn't no Black people be fucking with him!

Mumia: He'd be done. He'd be out of a career, frankly.

Marc: Right! Now, of course, this speaks to our community's own shame and anxiety around sexual identity and sexual abuse. But it also brings me back to my other question: How do we regard Black female bodies?

Mumia: We don't regard them very much. And unfortunately, as time goes forward, less so. You know, we love the ideal, but we don't love the real. I mean, when you're talking about R. Kelly, the cat is an extraordinary tenor singer. Extraordinary. I went after him for singing "You remind me of my jeep," but the cat is one of the baddest singers to hit the mic. He really is. I just saw him on the "Soul Train Awards" and he lit it on fire. The guy's incredible...

Marc: Oh, he bodied that performance. I remember thinking, *Yo, he's amazing with this thing!* But at the same time, I felt something deeply problematic about him even having that opportunity. His genius has never been in question, but the fact that he has an opportunity to be back on the main stage without any gestures of contrition is so deeply troubling. But it also made me question my own sensibilities. I stopped buying his albums and critiqued him publicly, but would I have had a more intense and genuinely indignant response if an artist were outed as a White supremacist? But there's something about this terrain of Black female bodies that makes it so easily forgivable. Same thing goes for Chris Brown. Our community was so quick to forgive him for abusing Rihanna. In fact, many people were saying, "Rihanna must have done something terrible to Chris to make him do that." It's like we were trying to find a way to justify his behavior rather than hold him accountable. And I'm not on no self-righteous shit. My response to their scandals hasn't been perfect either.

Mumia: Several years ago, I got a boatload of information from sista-supporters who objected to a piece I'd written saying that after his rape conviction, I was still a Mike Tyson fan. The thing is, I never believed he was guilty of rape, but of having an absolutely incompetent defense at trial. I also think Mike lacked the social vocabulary to communicate with girls because he grew up in places and ways where that kind of communication wasn't learned. That said, rape ain't hardly, and ain't never been, cool. Of all the people in the United States, Blacks, both men and women, should be clear on that! So my responses have hardly been perfect either. We struggle through these things.

In my own relationships with Black women, I've had to ask, "How DEEP is my love?"

Marc: Word. And this thing doesn't stop at the level of social criticism. It permeates our own personal relationships. Very recently, I've had to come to terms with my own relationships with Black women. I've had to examine how my politics and beliefs are often betrayed by my behaviors. I've had to look at my patterns of dishonesty, fear and emotional distance. I wrestle with my own contradictions and I have to ask, "How deep is my love?"

Mumia: I think all Black men in this society have to come to grips with that; me, you, all of us. I know me. Listen, man. I got more issues than the *Village Voice*. When I was younger, I was a straight up *ho*.

Marc: Word?

Mumia: I ain't gonna fake this thing, Marc. I was a ho! I couldn't—nah, I ain't gonna say that—I *wouldn't* say no. I ain't proud of it, but there it is, man.

Marc: Man, Mu, you have no idea how much I can relate. I have spent much of my adult life doing the same thing. I'm just coming to terms with how emotionally, not to mention physically, dangerous I was being.

Mumia: Me too! It took me years to peep that this was a hole in myself—an emptiness—that couldn't be filled that way.

Marc: Right. That's exactly how I felt. And now, as I've gotten older, my promiscuity has turned into an equally dangerous kind of serial monogamy. I keep entering and leaving relationships, trying to find a kind of peace and security and affirmation that I simply can't find in another person. Like you said, there's an emptiness that just can't be filled externally. That goes back to the whole self-love thing that we were discussing earlier. Self-love is not just about appreciating our physical features, though that's necessary. It's about appreciating the intrinsic worth of our very selves, our very souls. We have to know that we are worthy of giving and receiving love. It's like that Floetry song "Supastar": "Love isn't something that you earn, it's deserved / Love is something I can give 'cause I'm worth it." That's become my affirmation. I hope to really own that notion one day.

Mumia: That's why we have to turn inward and start understanding ourselves better. As men, it's easy to ignore the internal stuff. But if we don't address it, we'll just be out there.

Marc: I agree. But at the same time that we look inward, we must be willing to be transparent and vulnerable with our partners about where we are. After all—and I've only recently come to understand this—these journeys that we take come at a price to the people who love us. If we truly love them, we have to include them.

Mumia: But we often don't. Like I said, we love the ideal. We don't love the real. And here's the really crazy thing about it: I don't know a Black man that doesn't love his mama.

Marc: Of course.

Mumia: And I mean love her beyond all else. But when it comes to other sisters, that love does not transfer. And that's the crazy thing because it can even be your baby's mama. You know what I mean? And you'll look at your mama one way and you look at another woman a different way. Part of that is our culture. I mean, if someone told me in 1968 that in 30 to 40 years young boys were gonna be walking around talking about how they want to be pimps, I'd have either laughed or punched them. And we have inculcated into our culture, our music, our dress, our speech and our thought patterns some of the most reprehensible ideas and ideations about women that can be imagined. What is more fundamentally predatory than thinking about women from a pimp perspective? It's capitalism at its worse stage, where a woman is product.

Marc: Right. We're literally objectifying them. And we live within a dominant culture that normalizes that kind of hateful practice. In the past decade, we've seen the pimp become a normalized figure within the realm of popular culture. We've had TV shows called "Pimp My Ride" and energy drinks called "Pimp Juice." By sanitizing the pimp, we've managed to take the sting out of a practice that hinges upon the exploitation, abuse and often destruction of female bodies.

Mumia: When I see this pimpism that is so much a part of Black popular culture now, I think of how kids sometimes reflect the most unsavory parts of us. While pimpism goes against our rhetoric, I wonder if it doesn't pluck the string of our desires.

Marc: Wow! Say more about that.

Mumia: While the veterans of the '60s generation knew enough of feminism to know that this was exploitation, one can't deny that there is an allure, a magnetism, that appeals to something in us. And I think it's the hidden idealized as sexual object, not partner. I think we fantasize about women as objects of desire, but also subjected to the whim of money, thus disempowered by the indirect power of the market. Of course, it's all illusion. And worse, it's commerce.

Marc: That connects to an earlier point you were making about loving certain kinds of women and not others. If we're talking about love—I mean love for real, for real—then even when you put a woman on that pedestal, even when you have the idea of the woman as queen or Virgin Mother, whatever it is, that's still a dehumanizing position. Richard Iton calls it the "bitch-queen complex," where every woman is either viewed as mother of civilization or she's just some trick up the street. It denies them the kind of complexity that all human beings have. I think that our humanity actually rests between those two extremes, but we don't even allow that possibility for women. And I think that refusal disfigures our expectations and undermines our relationships.

Mumia: It's more perverse than that. Feminists back in the '70s talked about the hag and the crone and how men projected all the evil in the universe on elder women.

Marc: Ah, that's interesting.

Mumia: That's the history of Europe. And in many cases, it's the presence of Africa in some senses. But the real deal is this: We sneer at those who are most responsible for every living being on the planet. You know, before there was Adam there was Eve. You know what I'm saying? That's one of Huey's essays. You know, because every time I think about John Africa, I remember something he told a group of us many years ago. And he said, "If folks have to rely on men to give birth, the human race would die quick." And women recreate the world not just every day but thousands of times every day, every minute. They recreate the world, one by one. If you're lucky, sometimes in twos. And they almost die. It is more than a labor of love. It's a labor of life and sometimes death. And you know, we have created in many countries and in many parts of the world hells on earth for those beings who not only brought us forth, but who continue the human species.

Is it possible for us to love each other deeply and fully, as a community, if we haven't created INCLUSIVE, and loving spaces for gay, lesbian, bisexual, and transgendered brothers and sisters?

Marc: What about those love relationships that don't produce children? Particularly, let's think about gay and lesbian relationships. One of the most fascinating things to me about the 2008 election was the way that Black folk piled into the voting booths in record numbers to vote for Barack Obama, but many in California also voted for Proposition 8, which effectively ended gay marriage in the state. Is it possible for us to love each other deeply and fully, not just in terms of romantic relationships but as a community, if we haven't created full, inclusive and loving spaces for gay, lesbian, bisexual and transgender brothers and sisters?

Mumia: Is it possible? Yes. Is it probable? No. Our people are still primarily tied to our churches with a thousand ropes. We populate churches or mosques, which have, at their core, teachings that demonize gay, lesbian and transgender brothers and sisters. That's why so many dudes are "undercover" and why we get shocked so often by the sexual peccadilloes in the pulpit, or minaret for that matter. We are really quite conservative in that manner. But ultimately, if there is no love for all of us in these joints, then they will cease to function.

Marc: I agree with that. I would even go further and say that it's not even *possible* to have a truly loving community that doesn't include LGBT brothers and sisters. So what's the next step? How do we love each other more fully?

Mumia: You know what, Marc? We have to either love each other with all the force of our nature or we cease to be. It's as simple as that.

Marc: The stakes are really that high, huh?

Mumia: Absolutely. If we accept that we live in a profoundly White supremacist state, then we live in a soup that doesn't love us at a deep, fundamental level. If we don't actively, deeply and honestly love each other, with all our frailties, shortcomings, and, yes, our *issues*, then we will vanish from the earth. I believe that. I believe that love is a force, the most powerful in the world. It holds it together. And when people live, for years, apart from that force, they exile themselves from existence. The greatest act of liberation is love. The greatest act of revolution is love. And the greatest act of resistance that Black people can do is love each other with all the force we can muster. This is not about religion or creed or even politics. It's about life. I think it is love that enriches life, which gives color to life, and makes it worth living. Therefore, that love must be inclusive, or else, it will split and fray, and rend itself from itself. The first humans to turn their heads to the sky were Blacks. Thus all that lives is of that inheritance. We should love it all with vigor and give a new rebirth to the world.

FOR YOUR LIBRARY

The Fire Next Time, James Baldwin

Teachings on Love, Thich Nhat Hanh

All About Love, *Rock My Soul* and *Salvation*, bell hooks

Their Eyes Were Watching God, Zora Neale Hurston

Decoded, Jay-Z and dream hampton

Strength to Love, Martin Luther King, Jr.

Beloved, Toni Morrison

Methodology of the Oppressed, Chela Sandoval

For Colored Girls Who have Considered Suicide When the Rainbow is Enuf, Ntozake Shange

Jesus and the Disinherited, Howard Thurman

CHAPTER 8

Are We Not Men? Exploring Black Masculinity

Without question, Black males are in the midst of a crisis. From employment to education to mass incarceration, Black men are forced to confront a range of issues that severely undermine our life chances. These conditions are directly connected to particular conceptions of what it means to be designated "Black" and "male" within this society. In this conversation, we unpack the complex meanings of Black masculinity, both within and outside of the Black community, and examine their impact on the social, political and emotional wellbeing of both Black men and women. Although we disagree on many dimensions of the subject, we agree that we must collectively imagine and construct new and healthier models of Black masculinity.

Marc: We've spoken a lot about the role of Black men in society. I don't think we can have a serious conversation about Black men without discussing the idea of masculinity. From your standpoint, what is masculinity?

Mumia: I think that masculinity is something that's been projected and forced onto us. I say that generally, with respect to White, Black, Latino and Asian people. To be male in this society is to accept, to some degree, the construct of the "American man." That means being aggressive, domineering, boastful, outspoken and arrogant. This is the only construct that we have in America until people choose to deconstruct it and build another. It's planted deep in the psyche of all males in this country.

Marc: I agree. And it's also planted within the psyches of women. Like White supremacy, dangerous notions of masculinity are something that affects all of us and undermines all of our humanity. In your estimation, how does this idea of masculinity intersect with race? In other words, is there a distinctive thing that can be called "Black masculinity"?

Mumia: Some people, given their specific history, have had to develop other ways of coping, looking at, and living in the world. Thus "Black masculinity" developed negatively as a counter-identity to "White masculinity," for we could not function as White men in a profoundly Negrophobic environment. This was where Black nationalist and anti-colonialist identities emerged. They come from the experiences of alienation and oppression.

Marc: So you think that there's a fundamental difference between White masculinity and Black masculinity?

Mumia: Absolutely. The way Black men look at masculinity is completely different than other men in this culture of America. We have had to defend it unlike other people. We have been subjected to sexual violence, forced to do things in the name of the master and forced to see things being done to those we loved.

Is there a way to imagine MASCULINITY outside the framework of oppression?

Marc: I agree that the intersection of race and gender politics produces a distinctive "Black masculinity." I also agree that historical traumas have contributed greatly to the conceptions of masculinity that we're forced to negotiate these days. At the same time, I wonder what it means for us to frame Black masculinity within a context of emasculation. To me, the idea that masculinity is a thing that can be defiled or stripped away from Black men through sexual violence or the loss of our ability to deploy power and control over women and children is itself problematic. Is there a way to imagine masculinity outside the framework of oppression?

Mumia: For the sake of our mental, societal and communal health, there has to be. We have to do the hard work of redefining what masculinity means, so that we live in ways that are more life-affirming and whole for those people whom we love, and who love us. Haki Madhubuti is trying to do this in several of his latest books. He's trying to create a way of thinking, acting and being that promotes a holistic, more positive role for men in the Black community.

Marc: I think that one of the big problems with our understanding of Black masculinity is that it has been so intimately linked to patriarchy. As we were discussing earlier, so many of us attribute manhood to the ability to dominate and control things. I can't help but think that our attempts at affirming and performing masculinity are merely efforts to further normalize male dominance. And the thing is, the whole Black community buys into this idea to a large extent. All across Black life—in our movies, in our churches, in our barbershops—you hear people praying for the day that Black men are "allowed to be men" again. We wax nostalgic about the days when Black men "handled their business" in the household and in their romantic relationships. Hell, you even hear that kind of stuff coming from the hardcore Right, as conservative critics disingenuously clamor for the "repair of the Black family."

Mumia: Well, how could we not? When I hear critiques of Black patriarchy, whether it comes from the so-called Left or the Right, I'm actually angered.

Marc: Why?

Mumia: Because, in truth, Black men are perhaps the least patriarchal in this society.

Marc: Wow. That's a hell of a statement. I don't know about that one, big homie!

Mumia: It's true! Because, in our experience, Black women have been the providers for at least two generations, given the official and practiced exclusion of Black men from many areas of economic endeavor. I think, in fact, that we've been practicing a kind of faux-patriarchy, or perhaps a petit-patriarchy, for we have not had the wealth or access to capital or property that makes such a patriarchy possible. And, you better know, whoever brings home the bacon was boss at home. And far too often, or far too inconsistently, that was not the brotherman. According to my research and study, Black women far outstrip dudes in college attendance, graduation, grad school and advanced degrees. I saw a study a few years ago from the Joint Center for Black Political and Economic Studies. The study's numbers were off the chain when it came to Black boys dropping out of high school and college. If memory serves, I think it said that the highest percentage of Black male college students were admitted for their performance in sports departments! Now, I'm not saying that some dudes don't act cuckoo in the homes, getting bossy and what-not. But again, even this is behavior that is copied in imitation of what they see and hear and absorb from the culture—it's like an exaggerated expression—that's reflective, not of patriarchy, but the very lack of power. It's really bullying. I mean, for

Black men act dominant sometimes, to mask our lack of domination in the fields where it REALLY matters: economics, politics, academics and other spaces where real power gets transacted.

real, where do we dominate? The basketball court? The prison block? The street? The bedroom? Truth is, we don't dominate many of those places, so we act dominant sometimes, I think, to mask our lack of domination in the fields where it really matters: economics, politics, academics and other spaces where power gets transacted.

Marc: I have to disagree, bruh. By that logic, poor White people could say that they don't have the institutional power to be racist. Of course, we'd challenge such a claim by pointing to the power of White skin privilege even in the midst of economic disadvantage. The same thing holds for Black men when it comes to patriarchy. We may not have the institutional power to control the broader social world, but we certainly have the power to be oppressive within our own communities. And when you look in our churches, our homes and our broader culture, that's exactly what you see. To me, that's patriarchy.

Another issue is the relationship between masculinity and sexuality. We've constructed a notion of masculinity that is defined by hypersexuality and compulsory heterosexuality. Even thinking about the conversation that we had about sexual promiscuity, how much of our behavior was criticized by our community? Now if we had been women having that much sex, we'd have been castigated. If we'd have been having sex with men instead of women, we'd be outcasts.

Mumia: You ain't never lied! But again, how much is this media and cultural hype? While that notion is out there, we didn't put it out there. Rather, we played according to a script written by other forces. I grew up listening to dudes who were crooning to sisters, expressing their longing, love and desire to them. Cats like Smokey, The Temptations, Teddy Pendergrass, Luther…

Marc: Umm, Luther?

Mumia: Okay, maybe Luther wasn't singing to sisters, but we didn't know that when we first heard him!

Marc: Okay, fair enough!

Mumia: That said, if we ain't truly free then we can't freely be whomever we opt to be. That means, as we are still not free, we can't engage freely in whatever sexuality we feel drawn to. Also, Black people, even among the Black bourgeoisie, care about what White folks think and say about us. So I think you'll find less freedom, at least sexually, for those who live and work around Whites, for they have far more constraints on their behavior. So bottom line: If we ain't free, then we can't be free sexually.

Marc: I hear that. At the same time, we have to find ways to engage in anti-oppressive behaviors and practices even while facing tremendous oppression. It's the only pathway to freedom. Unfortunately, the Black community still fails to truly accept gay identities. Why do you think it's been such a challenge for us? Where do you stand on the issue?

Mumia: I think it's really what I just said. We ain't free so we can't live freely in any real human dimension. After all, what's more emblematic of human freedom than human sexuality? The churches, mosques and synagogues have been policing this stuff for centuries. Why? Because they recognized its power. And I mean that more from a political than a religious standpoint, because religious structures are ultimately political. In fact, 700 years ago, they were telling kings and queens what to do and who to do it with! So it comes down to freedom, freedom to be fully human in all ways that are meaningful to human beings—as opposed to human-led institutions. Ultimately, that's what it comes down to: Human relationships.

Marc: I think that our families, our communities, and our political movements will never be whole or healthy until we create space for people to be gay, lesbian, bisexual or transgender. A key example of this idea is the whole "down low" phenomenon. Rather than thinking about the DL as evidence of the complex range of sexual identities that operate within communities, we've allowed the media to frame the issue in typically pathological terms. Suddenly the 'DL' male becomes the latest version of the all-too-familiar Black sexual predator. Despite all of the scientific medical evidence to the contrary, the popular media quickly spread the myth that DL men were responsible for the breakdown of "traditional" relationships and the spread of HIV/AIDS among Black women.

Mumia: I don't know if you recall, but Huey P. Newton spoke out, back in the 1970s, about gay liberation. He didn't just mention it. He said something like, "We, the Black Panther Party, support gay liberation just as we support women's liberation." He saw it as part of the struggle for human liberation. I have to admit that, at the time when we heard that, it didn't go down too well among the membership. Dudes looked at each other like, *"WTF?"* Yet and still, it was the most forward position of any radical and revolutionary movement of the period, and reflected Huey's keen thinking on issues before his time. So even in a movement perceived as "masculinist," there were these insights. But, you know what? Movements change consciousness, they change history and they can transform societies.

Marc: It's also interesting how this conversation happens exclusively within Black quarters. When New Jersey Governor Jim McGreevey admits that he

Huey P. Newton saw gay liberation as part of the struggle for HUMAN liberation.

was a "gay American" who was having affairs with men despite being married to a woman, no one said he was on the "down low." When the movie *Brokeback Mountain* comes out, featuring two undercover gay White cowboys, no one calls it a "down low" film. Part of that has to do with the outside world, but much of it has to do with Black homophobia. I'm not suggesting that there isn't homophobia in every racial group, but it seems that we create even less space for diverse Black sexual identities within our community. I think this is directly connected to our rigid and dangerous conceptions of masculinity. There's simply no room to be anything other than straight.

Mumia: It's interesting that you mentioned McGreevey because I think there are more similarities than differences when it comes to Black and non-Black dudes when it comes to homosexuality. McGreevey, as a politician, wasn't just a dude who "discovered" his gay identity. He was a politician who openly opposed any efforts by his government to accommodate gay people, or the reality of that life. In short, he was a political enemy to his hidden self and others of that persuasion. And that, I think, was because politics is a public performance of imagery, not substance. That's why dude was married to a beautiful woman. I don't want to get into her space but, how didn't she know? She couldn't tell? Was dude playin' both sides of the disco? I think people are so terrified of being outed that they hide such things from themselves. So, in essence, this guy, ostensibly the most powerful man in the state, wasn't really free either. How much less free is Tyrone, who lives in the heart of the ghetto, whose mom goes to a homophobic church? Let's be real!

Marc: To me, the only way out of this painful space is for the Black community to create new sites of possibility for sexuality. Until we acknowledge and accept a range of sexual identities, we're creating the very closets that we stigmatize men for hiding in. Now, to be clear, there's absolutely no excuse for lying to your intimate partner about your sexual desires and activities. None at all. Everyone should have a right to make decisions for themselves rather than have someone else make it for them through their dishonesty. But that honesty must be demanded of everyone, not just gay or bisexual men. We all must be transparent. Still, until we create space within our real and imagined communities to accommodate queer identities, we're going to have problems.

Mumia: Marc, your call for sexual transparency flies in the face of a culture of masking, where we had to literally use codes to communicate with each other. How can we be expected to speak our thoughts about sexuality, especially gay sexuality, when we've never been allowed to speak our thoughts?

Marc: But isn't honesty healthier?

Mumia: Yes, more honesty in such matters would safeguard more partners. If you truly care for someone, you don't want to hurt them. But let me say this, if any people are able to achieve such a task, it's Black folks.

Marc: Why do you say that, Mu?

Mumia: Because of our historical and contemporary role in American life, as the measure of what freedom really looks like and means. In the book, *Playing in the Dark: Whiteness and the Literary Imagination*, Toni Morrison wrote, "Africanism is the vehicle by which the American self knows itself as not enslaved, but free." In law, the very notion of freedom emerges, not from the opening sections of the Constitution, not from the Declaration of Independence, but from the Reconstruction Amendments: the 13th, 14th and 15th Amendments to the Constitution. It literally made millions of people—who weren't Black for the most part—citizens. Women, gay folks, Jewish folks, Mormons, the physically disabled—you name it, and they became citizens because Black folks were said to be. The same thing is possible on the issue of sexuality if we use the tools of our culture.

Marc: I agree that Black people have always been central to the liberation of all American citizens. That's why it was so sad in November 2008 to see so many Black people pile into voting booths in record number to elect a Black president, while simultaneously voting to end gay marriage in California through Proposition 8. At the same time, this is not just about gay and bisexual men, but about straight brothers and sisters too. After all, our collective homophobia limits the possibilities for how all of us can engage the world and each other. You mentioned earlier how your father would hug and kiss you. Sadly, that's a rare occurrence in our community, largely because of the cultural scripts that are pre-written for Black men in society. There's very little room for men to show love, appreciation or affection for other men. Sure, in church we can drop down on our knees and shake and cry and praise the male body of Jesus. But other than that, where can men show such emotion for another man? Where, other than on a basketball court or football field, can we hug or otherwise physically affirm our affection for one another? The possibilities are so narrow that it's depressing.

Our collective homophobia LIMITS the possibilities for how all of us can engage the world and each other.

Mumia: You know, what we bring in thought, we follow through in speech and we complete in action. I remember as clear as day a time when I was walking down Columbia Avenue in North Philly in the summer of 1969. I was greeting and being greeted by brothers and sisters just walking down the street: "How you doin' brotha?" "Hello, sista!" and so on. It was a beautiful thing! Then I ran into a dope fiend boy, nodding at the bus stop. He came out of a nod, looked up at me, and I said, "How you doin, brotha?" This dude curled up his lip and spat out, "I ain't yo' brotha, nigga!" with so much venom that it rocked me. I bit my tongue and looked at him. He fell back into a swoon. The experience taught me, firsthand, how poisonous drugs were, for they killed our spirits. And for far too many, drugs doped out our capacity for compassion and love of our people. I'm using that example to show the absence of love. After all, if you hate yourself, you're unable to love others. When we greet each other in loving terms, with a loving spirit, it usually pulls out a similar vibration in others if you're sincere. If we love each other in thought, and communicate that in speech, we put a vibration into action that'll almost always be reciprocated. We call each other everything but "brother" these days: "dog," "homie," "boy," "nigga." How did "brother" get lost? My old man hugged and kissed my brothers and me. We hug and kiss our children—boys and girls. But I think most of us have been unloved so long that we fear it. It's strange to us. It's not "real" to very many of us. We gotta make it real. In our hearts, in our mouths and in our hugs.

Marc: Well, one of the places where masculinity is radically re-imagined and performed in different ways is inside of prisons. It seems to me that prison serves as a space where the normal scripts of gender and sexuality get edited, where we see new possibilities for what it means to be masculine. For example, in prison you see men having sex with men without compromising their "manhood" or "masculinity" in the same way that they would out in the world. How do you see this idea?

Because prison strips people of so much, it allows dudes to really CONNECT with other dudes in different ways, most of which are non-sexual.

Mumia: Marc, I think it's more similar to street life than you think. It's about power and domination. In that way, it mimics male/female sex. And it *definitely* impacts notions of "masculinity" and/or "manhood." It is actually another false form of hypermasculinity in my view. The man who is the "bottom," the one being penetrated is the woman, so it echoes a dynamic that governs the "free" world. That said, because prison strips people of so much, it allows dudes to really connect with other dudes in different ways, most of which are non-sexual. These connections have meaning and caring that spans generations. I've written before about guys in prison calling me "papa" and how uncomfortable it made me, because I was separated from my own children. But I learned that guys call you that if you truly, honestly teach them, for you are performing a function that they wish their true fathers did. You became a kind of stand-in, as an older fellow. So "teacher" becomes a form of masculinity that still has resonance in the joint.

Detachment from a full range of emotions reinforces and normalizes a culture of violence, not just among men but with women too.

Marc: I think that what you just said is so important. By calling you papa, those brothers are able to explore and discover emotions that were previously off-limits to them. They are able to heal some of their wounds. You know, we always talk about how emotional women are, but the truth is that men are emotional too. The only difference is that men are taught only to show the emotion of anger. As a result, we are not equipped to articulate when we're feeling inadequate, insecure or scared. Instead, we funnel all of those feelings and emotions through unhealthy expressions of anger.

Mumia: Anger is the only socially respected form of emotion that men may feel. Unless you are a Black man, in which case that anger cannot be directed at someone non-Black. You know, it reminds me of "Star Trek."

Marc: How so?

Mumia: Well, in "Star Trek," the Vulcans were famously unemotional when, in fact, they felt all the emotions. They just suppressed them. Black men are taught early to suppress their fears, their pains, their loves and their "inappropriate" angers. This often makes us crazy, for suppression is just another form of repression and alienation. You end up splitting yourself into something other than yourself. This also causes trauma for loved ones, who often fail to learn how to love because they

Eighty percent of Black women suffer from fibroid disease. There's no disease that would afflict 80 percent of Black men that Black women wouldn't know about.

feel that they've never been loved. Because our people suffered such tough lives, we regarded sentiment as weakness. We just dried our tears and kept on stepping.

Marc: This kind of detachment from the full range of emotions also reinforces and normalizes a culture of violence, not just among men but with women as well. Intimate partner violence and sexual assault are extremely prevalent within our community, just like in others, and I can't help but think it's connected to the way we think and talk about our physical relationships to women. Earlier, we talked about how the mainstreaming of the pimp within public culture has contributed to the normalization of sexual exploitation of women and physical violence. But let's also think about the phrases that ordinary men—not just pimps—use to talk about sex: "I'm gonna hit that," "I'm gonna beat it up," "I'm gonna pound that." Now, I'm not trying to be prudish or foreclose on any romantic or erotic possibilities. After all, there might be some nights when you and your partner want it to go down like that...

Mumia: I hear you!

Marc: But it seems deeply troubling to me, scary even, that these are the *only* metaphors that we use to describe our sexual activity. By framing it exclusively through the language of physical violence, I worry that we normalize this behavior and desensitize ourselves to the harsh realities of it.

Mumia: Damn. That's absolutely true. I've never even thought about it that way.

Marc: That's just it. We don't have to think about it. It's part of what scholars like R. L'Heureux Lewis, Jewel Woods and Mark Anthony Neal and others refer to as "Black male privilege."

Mumia: Black male privilege? Hmm, that's an interesting phrase. How are you thinking about this? Give me some examples.

Marc: Well, the fundamental idea is that Black men must confront the ways that they benefit from their respective positions, particularly in relationship to Black woman, in various spheres of life. For example, as Black men, we don't have to choose our race over our gender when engaging in political action. Or thinking about the dating thing, we can be polygamous and polyamorous with little social repercussion. The best example, though, came from Mark Anthony Neal when we were on a panel together. He asked how many of the brothers in the audience knew that 80 percent of all Black women suffer from some form of fibroid disease. Very few brothers knew. Mark then pointed out that there is no disease that would afflict 80 percent of Black men that Black women would be largely ignorant of. To me, this exemplifies Black male privilege. Like White privilege, it's about having the prerogative not to know or care about the concerns of the "other" group with little or no material consequence.

It is deeply troubling and scary even that the only metaphors that we use to describe sexual activity are violent.

Mumia: When I heard you talk about 80 percent, my reaction was "Wow." Because I've known women in my family who have had that situation, but 80 percent? Initially, I thought your idea of Black male privilege was misplaced. Thinking about that 80 percent, I have to reconsider and rethink that issue. Kind of like I said before, I think we have a faux-Black male privilege, oc-

I believe the whole idea of masculinity is irreparably damaged. The term is too rooted in patriarchy, homophobia and violence.

casioned and indeed enabled by the sheer paucity of Black men in light of the depredations wrought by the prison industrial complex. But again, Neal's point about fibroid problems in our mothers, wives, daughters and sisters is stunning. How could we not know something like that? This is only possible if we, collectively and separately, don't care enough to know. I must submit to your argument. And once accepting it, I have to acknowledge that it is a perspective that poses a serious danger to women in our community. I initially thought it as a kind of intellectual construct that didn't reflect real, lived reality. I can't say that anymore.

Marc: Well let me take it a step further. I've come to believe that this whole idea of "masculinity" is fundamentally flawed and irreparably damaged. The term itself is so deeply rooted in traditions of patriarchy, homophobia and various forms of violence that it is not salvageable. Or even if it is salvageable, it isn't worth our collective energy. Our goal shouldn't be to rescue masculinity, but to eliminate it. In the same way that anti-racist activists say that "Whiteness" must be eliminated and that Whites must become "race traitors," I believe that we must do the same as Black men. We must destroy this idea of Black masculinity and come up with something different. Simply put, what we've been doing just isn't working.

FOR YOUR LIBRARY

Go Tell It on the Mountain, **James Baldwin**

Beyond the Down Low, **Keith Boykin**

Race Men, **Hazel V. Carby**

Black Feminist Thought, **Patricia Hill Collins**

Invisible Man, **Ralph Ellison**

We Real Cool, **bell hooks**

Sweet Tea, **E. Patrick Johnson**

Black Men: Obsolete, Single, Dangerous?, **Haki Madhubuti**

Cool Pose, **Richard Majors**

Why I Hate Abercrombie & Fitch, **Dwight A. McBride**

When Chickenheads Come Home to Roost, **Joan Morgan**

New Black Man, **Mark Anthony Neal**

CHAPTER 9

Matters of Life and Death

In this final conversation, we discuss the looming presence of death in our friendship, our personal lives and our community. Like all of our exchanges, this one occurred against the backdrop of death row, where Mumia continues to literally fight for his life. At the same time, we were still struggling to deal with the sudden deaths of our dear friends and comrades Gil Scott Heron and Manning Marable, as well as several other loved ones. Still, in the true spirit of African people, our painful conversation about death was quickly transformed into a meditation on subversive joy, revolutionary love and boundless hope.

Marc: It's impossible to talk to you without being reminded that you're on death row. When I visit you, we're separated by glass. The closest thing we have to touching is putting our fists to the glass. When we talk on the phone, any sense of comfort is interrupted by an operator reminding me that I'm talking to an inmate at a "correctional institution." I can only imagine how intense those reminders are for you on the other side of the bars. What's it like to be constantly surrounded by the shadow of death?

Mumia: You are unable to forget it, either on the phone, or in daily life, because it's all-encompassing. In reality, there are very few similar extremities in life. But the sad truth of the matter is, like millions of Black men, we are always surrounded by the "shadow of death." I mean this sincerely. I know, when I was a teenager and a member of the Black Panther Party, I certainly felt that way–especially after the conspiracy and murders of Deputy Chairman Fred Hampton and Captain Mark Clark. Fred was killed in his bed. I, like quite a few Panthers, expected to join him when our homes or offices got raided. So that was a part of my consciousness from a very young age. Also, perhaps more commonly, you can't tell me that guys don't feel deep, existential dread when they see a cop car in the rearview mirror. They don't know whether it's gonna be a Rodney King thing or something worse.

Marc: I hear that. But at the same time, you are facing something far more intense and far more immediate than the rest of us. I know that there's a political dimension to being on death row, but there's something far more personal going on that I think many people miss. From a personal perspective, what's the toughest part of being on death row?

Mumia: Being away from my wife and my children. Being away from the people I love and who love me. Without question, that's the toughest part of all this. And it's not just tough on me. It's tough on them too. But you just have to do your best to stay in touch and to be there in all the ways that you can.

The WORST thing about being on death row is being away from my wife and children. But we hold together because of the depth of our love.

Marc: How have you managed to sustain your relationships? How have you been able to sustain bonds with your children when you've been away from them longer than you've been with them?

Mumia: It's hard, man. And, you know, it's especially hard because they were small when I left. But when the love is there, you can do it. I let my children know that, no matter what happens, dad is always gonna be there. They can feel my love.

Marc: Still, it must be hard to keep that love alive with all of the things the prisons do to kill it. To me, one of the worst parts is the non-contact visits, which are designed to destroy your outside relationships and kill your spirit. I've come to learn that there's something quintessentially human about the ability to touch, to hug, to kiss. To feel. It heals us. It feeds our souls. To take that away from a person is its own kind of death sentence. I remember in *Live From Death Row* when you talked about your 5-year-old daughter's first visit to the prison. She kept banging her little fists against the glass, demanding to know why she couldn't hug you or kiss you or sit on your lap. I know how painful that was for both of you.

Mumia: Absolutely. Her voice haunted me for a long time. It really reminds me of how this place is designed to kill your soul. But when the love is real and you really work on it, you can do it. No matter how old my kids get—and they're parents themselves now—I never stop making them handmade birthday cards. I never stop checking on them and letting them know how much I love them. That kind of love can cut through the glass. They can feel it. And so can my wife.

Marc: I know she does. I can remember a couple of times when you told me you had to cut our calls short. You were like, "I gotta talk to my honey. I miss her." You sounded like a schoolboy!

Mumia: Hey, man. That's how it is!

Marc: And I know she feels the same way. The love you two share is unbelievably strong.

No matter how old my kids get— and they're parents themselves now—I NEVER stop making them handmade birthday cards.
I NEVER stop checking on them and letting them know how much I love them. That kind of love can cut through the glass.

Mumia: Yeah, man. It ain't perfect, but it's real. It's strong. And it helps keep both of us going through all the madness of the life, including death row. It keeps me alive and gives me hope.

Marc: I feel that. And while all Black people aren't on death row, we certainly all face a collective despair that's rooted in various forms of death: social, cultural, economic and psychological. How do we as a people sustain any hope in the midst of all this suffering?

The love I share with my wife keeps me ALIVE on death row and gives me hope.

Mumia: In many ways, this is the gift and the curse of Blackness in America. We epitomize both hope and despair in one body, in one people. We are the exemplars of love, but we also exemplify despair. All humans suffer—it's part of our condition—but no people have experienced the kind of sustained suffering that Black people have experienced over the past 500 years.

Marc: I'm always reluctant to compare human suffering, but it's impossible to deny that Black folk have experienced an unprecedented level of physical, psychological and emotional pain. Our trauma runs so deep.

Mumia: But we've also found ways to rise above it. We've used the strength of the human spirit to resist.

Marc: But what is it that animates our spirits? After all, we live in a world that is so anti-life. From the reckless way that we destroy the environment, to the cruel ways that we treat animals, to our general indifference regarding the misery of fellow humans around the globe, we live in a pro-death culture. In the midst of that, how are we able to sustain a belief and investment in life?

Mumia: Our historical knowledge and experiences are sort of coded within our DNA. No people are as free in their spirit, happy-go-lucky and light as Black people. That's part of who we are. One day, a German activist wrote to me and asked me what it's like when guys on death row get together in the cages. I told her, "You'll hear some of the funniest shit you'd ever want to hear!"

Marc: That's so true. I remember the first time I visited you. I expected you to be this real serious dude. And, of course, that would have been cool. I don't expect a nigga on death row to be Richard Pryor.

Mumia: Right. I think a nigga on death row deserves a pass for being a little serious!

Marc: Word. But then I got there and you were the exact opposite! Within 20 minutes, you literally had me on the floor cracking up. You were telling stories and doing impersonations. I couldn't believe how ridiculously funny you were.

Mumia: Well, truth be told, I've always been a funny person. Of course, I know that people who read my work may not see that side. That's generally because I write about serious things and ideas.

Marc: But then there's that other side of you. You're hilarious.

Mumia: It's gallows humor, but it's funny! And it's not just me. There was a brother in here from North Philly named Kenyatta. This dude would have us crying, saying, "Please, stop" because our sides would be hurting, our heads would be hurting and snot would be running down our faces because he was that witty and clever. And he would do it with a blank look on his face.

Marc: That's the shit I'm talking about, man. There's a tragicomic sensibility in that. In the midst of absurdity, we're able to invoke a sense of joy. Whether it's making jokes while sitting on death row, singing sorrow songs while working on a slave plantation or everyday Black people living under hellish conditions, we've always managed to retrieve joy from a pile of social misery.

Mumia: I think it's an intensely human response, but it's also that we laugh to keep from crying. That is really who we are. That's why Blacks embody the desperation and the joy of life. That's how we were able to create the blues. That's why, when White folks created parodies of Black folks by putting on blackface, you had some Black actors who put tar on their face too! Like, *"I'm getting' paid, nigga!"* But when you look back at them

Whether it's making jokes while sitting on death row, singing sorrow songs while working on a slave plantation, or everyday Black people living under hellish conditions, we've always managed to retrieve JOY from a pile of social misery.

dudes, they were, during their time, some of the highest paid entertainers in Black America. In many ways, they were laughing all the way to the bank! They were also playing a kind of inside joke on White folks— by out-niggerin' the White minstrels—and dropping things that made people laugh and think.

Marc: Exactly! And I think the Blues tradition is essential for understanding how Black people have responded to our condition in America. I mean there's nothing more quintessentially tragicomic than the Blues.

You listen to songs like "Your Wife is Cheating on Us" and you hear how Black people respond to misfortune through irony, laughter and playfulness. It's important to understand, however, that this isn't just a superficial masking of pain. It's an assertion of a different level of humanity. It's a commitment to not becoming prisoner to despair. Unfortunately, some folks miss this point. They think that Black people are so busy smiling that we fail to address our real issues.

Mumia: But that's an external reading that does not dig deeply enough. The human condition has enough tragedy because we're the only beings that understand that we're mortal. We recognize the profundity of life and try to squeeze some life and some laughter out of it. It makes life worth living.

Marc: Exactly. And underneath that laughter is a deeper understanding of human possibility. Of course, we have to be fully aware of our past, of our current condition and of the very real obstacles that we face individually and collectively. We cannot ignore our pain or underestimate the intensity of our circumstance. We have an obligation to each other and ourselves to walk through the world with our eyes wide open. Still, to borrow from Howard Thurman, we don't have to be "prisoners of the event." We can opt to resist. We can opt to imagine another reality. We can hope.

Mumia: I think, other than perhaps Native Americans, Blacks in the United States have had the biggest purchase on hope. How could we survive otherwise? We had to see another tomorrow, when everything—*everything*—in the environment told us that the situation was/is/and will forever be hopeless. Think of the Dred Scott case, decided by the Supreme Court in 1857. It ruled that Black folks, whether slave or free, could never become citizens. It also said that even their descendents, free or not, could never enjoy the rights ascribed in the Constitution. Boy, talk about a recipe for hopelessness! Black folks, for the most part, just kept on stepping! We are people partly composed of hope. In many ways, it is who we are.

Marc: Historically, that's certainly been the case. More recently, though, many of us have responded to social misery with drugs and alcohol. Of course, there have always been stimulants and stuff in every community throughout history. In the last 30 to 40 years, though, they've become a primary mechanism for dealing with social misery and despair. It seems to me that, in some sense, we've set aside some of our healthier strategies and taken up these artificial forms of coping. They've led us into a very dangerous place.

Mumia: Well, yeah, 'cause what drugs are really about is escape. A false escape. It's escape from the horror and the misery of daily Black life. But after that high is over, "Welcome back to hell." You haven't changed that reality.

Marc: No doubt. I think that's why mental health care is so important. Unfortunately, we live in a culture that resists the use of counselors, therapists and psychologists. Of course, for Black people there's good reason. After all, the medical establishment hasn't been very good to us.

Mumia: Can you say Tuskegee? For millions of Blacks, especially those over a certain generation, our distrust of the medical establishment is profound and well-founded, for medicine was more often a tool of destruction than a science of health-provision. That's because we learned about the Tuskegee experiment, where doctors and nurses knowingly treated Black men infected with syphilis with placebos for decades.

Marc: No doubt. There's plenty of reason to be wary of the medical establishment, but the fact remains that we're walking around deeply wounded. In the absence of mental health care, we're opting to self-medicate through drugs and other self-destructive behaviors. We have to find ways of healing ourselves so that we can continue to change our collective condition and, on a more basic level, find the power to make it through the day.

Mumia: I think it echoes of the "Tuskegee effect," distrust of the medical establishment, of their drugs, their treatments and their integrity. In many ways, we search for alternatives, preferably from nature, to augment the system. Also, I think, for quite a few folks, the church functions as a mental health center, you follow me? That's one of the few places Blacks appear to be whole.

Marc: It seems that one of the ways that you escape from the hells of death row is through your dreams. In your writing, particularly in *Live from Death Row,* you mention your dreams a lot and talk about them as a kind of refuge from day-to-day life.

Mumia: You know, Freud said dreams are the royal road to the unconscious. For me, they are the roads to inner freedom, for my life, is completely unbounded and unhindered in the realm of dreams. They are completely uninhibited and fantastical.

Marc: What do you dream about?

Mumia: You will not believe this. I rarely write about it and rarely still talk about it because I know it will freak a lot of people out. But you ask and here it go!

Living on death row has meant I rely on my dreams as roads to inner FREEDOM because in them my life, is completely unbounded and unhindered.

Marc: Uh oh!

Mumia: I travel the world. Many times I travel back to my memories. I'm surprised at how often I'll dream about something like Plainfield, Vermont, where I went to college, because it's a beautiful spot. I've dreamt about being animals, different genders even different races.

Marc: Damn.

Mumia: I surprise myself, like, *"Damn where did that come from?"*

Marc: Did you dream like that before you where incarcerated?

Mumia: I don't think I did. I don't have any memory of it. I think this is a direct reflection of the repression of incarceration. So now, in my dreams, I exercise a kind of über-freedom. And I remember once, man, dreaming that I was in the ocean as a porpoise or shark, or some kind of underwater life. And you know it shocked me that I dug it! But sometimes when I'm into it, I don't dig it.

Marc: What do you mean?

Mumia: Sometimes I'm so into my dreams that I don't know I'm dreaming. If I'm walking down the street, I *feel* the sun's heat. I sweat, you know? Or when I'm someone else, I'm not Mumia behind a mask. I'm that person. Living, walking and speaking in *their* voice, not mine!

Marc: Who else have you been in your dreams?

Mumia: Man, I've been everything: a White woman, an Asian woman, a White man!

Marc: A White man? Aw, shit! Nigga, you definitely dreaming then!

Mumia: That was a nightmare! Like, *"What the hell was that?"* Dreams are a refuge, but they're also a helluva way to travel.

Marc: I think that's fascinating. In many ways, dreams become one of the few safe spaces to exercise new forms of freedom. For example, there's no safe place in the physical world for you to "try on" the identity of an Asian woman. But in our dreams, we're safe to be whoever we want, however we want. At least if we are able to fully release our imaginations. But then you awake from those dreams. And when you do, you're still, for all intents and purposes, inside of a death camp. How do you deal with that reality?

Mumia: It used to be devastating to awake from such a dream to such a nightmare. But I think it fuels my work. It is a death camp, surrounded by dozens of men who are part of the same camp. So you work as well as you can to transform that situation. But, as I've suggested earlier, being Black in America ain't no piece of cake. I remember reading Huey's book *Revolutionary Suicide*. He said all of us are mortally ill and all of us will pass this phase of life. All of us will die. To read that when you're 15 is a hell of a wake-up call.

Marc: Shit, it's a hell of a wake-up call at any age!

Mumia: It really is. Americans, unlike people in more ancient cultures, rarely think about death. In Black America, we share that same kind of liberal illusion. It's an illusion because we've cleaned up death in many ways. We very rarely see that in our lives. Of course, there's an exception to that rule if you live in the 'hood. I remember seeing it when I was like 7 or 8 years old. A brother on the playground got into a fight with another brother. I

Death has always felt so close to me. I've NEVER taken for granted that I'm alive.

ran out on the blacktop and one of the men was just laying there, almost dead. Our neighborhoods are different than most of America's.

Marc: Growing up in Philly, I also became accustomed to seeing and hearing about death at an early age. As I got older, it only got worse. I've lost so many friends, family and oldheads to senseless killings. Some of them I saw firsthand. Death has always felt so close to me. I've never taken for granted that I'm alive. That kind of reality has a particular kind of impact on our psyches.

Mumia: I agree, but I think it has dual impacts, both negative and positive. It forces many of us to deal with this at an early age. But it also charges our lives with more meaning, color and verve.

Marc: It also makes us more mature. As vulnerable people, we have come to terms with the inevitability of death. It allows us to have a more mature stance toward death, as opposed to the Western preoccupation with avoiding, denying and even stigmatizing death. In the West, we tend to behave as if death is something that we can run from. We tend to act as if the only people who are dying are the elderly and those who suffer from illnesses like cancer or HIV/AIDS. The truth is that we're all dying. We're all death-eligible. Life is a terminal illness.

Mumia: That's right.

Marc: And it's sexually transmitted!

Mumia: True!

Marc: So for Black folk, the perverseness and pervasiveness of death culture has certainly added to our collective trauma. But, at the same time, it has created a certain kind of courage and strength.

Mumia: I actually think it's done even more than that for Black people. In this culture, we have a real *joie de vivre*, a real joy of life, that is infectious. It's what animates our music. It's what animates how we walk through the street. It even allows us to dare death.

Marc: How often do you think about death?

[Here, Mumia pauses for a long time and then sighs deeply.]

Mumia: Every day. Every day.

Marc: Damn.

Mumia: Yeah.

Marc: Does it get easier? After all, you've been forced to come to terms with death in a whole different way because of your circumstance. Does that make it easier to negotiate death? Are you scared of it?

Mumia: You have to be fearless with it because you don't control it. You really do not control it. So I don't waste days. I don't waste time. When people really get a grip of the kind of work I do, they see how hard I work. Even my play is work 'cause my play is drawing, painting or writing music. But you know that's a lot of work. I don't have no computer in here. I'm writing notes by hand.

Marc: I can attest to that. If I send you something to read or edit, you always turn it around within 24 hours. It's amazing to me how hard you're working in the midst of such unimaginable chaos. But I've also come to understand, I think, that you also find great pleasure in the work you're doing.

Mumia: Of course. It's relaxing and I get a great deal of joy out of it. But also, I don't waste time. I take time very seriously.

Marc: Yet you also find the time to explore new parts of yourself. Just in the last year alone, you've started to write operas. I thought you were teasing me when you first started explaining it. Then, after a while, I was like, *"This dude is serious!"*

Mumia: Well I'm a hard worker and, as you know from reading my books, a serious student. Several years ago, two sisters from Pittsburgh, Martha and Bariki, came up to see me. Somehow, in our conversation, we came across the subject of music. All of us agreed that we loved music, but when I told them I used to sing in a choir when I was a teenager I could tell they were somewhat skeptical. I don't think they could fully accept it in their idea of who "Mumia" was. So I sang several stanzas from memory of "Agnus Dei" and they sat there with their mouths open in shock. They didn't expect me to sing to them. Especially in Latin! So I explained that I was part of the best youth choir in the city, composed of dozens of youngsters, culled from schools across the city and my only regret, I said, was that I never learned how to read and write music. Martha asked, "How could you sing in that kind of choir, without learning how to read and write music?" I explained that I learned to memorize my part, the part for tenors, and the parts right before my parts. Then, one of the sisters turned to the other and essentially offered her services. I asked, "Are you serious?" She said, "I am if you are." I was. She was. She began coming up every week, teaching me note by note, staff by staff, with flash cards. It was a wonderful experience, that engaged me in something that was transformative. Before long, I was actually on my way to reading and understanding music. It was literally like opening a doorway into a whole new world.

Marc: Wow. That's the thing about you that amazes me: the strength of your spirit. I remember a couple of years ago when you called me after getting the latest decision from the Pennsylvania Supreme Court. It was bad news and you were breaking down the details to me. I was pissed off because the decision was bullshit. The more we talked and the more you explained, the more worked up I got. By the end of the conversation, I was nearly in tears. You were still calm, like, *"Marc it's gonna be alright, bro. We gonna battle this, we gonna beat this."* It wasn't until I got off the phone and chilled for a second that I was like, *"Yo, this nigga is on death row and he's cheering me up!"*

Mumia: You know what? This ain't just for you. I do this for everybody because I believe, on the one hand, that how we think does affect the real. On the other hand, and I learned this years ago from being with MOVE people, it's important to keep shit light. Because otherwise you'll get funked out and you'll be like Bill Tilley, a brother that got hung up at four in the morning. He killed himself because his health was fucked up and wasn't nothing coming legally. Four o'clock in the morning, he's strapped up.

Marc: Do you ever get that impulse, Mu? Do you ever have the impulse to be like, *"Fuck it,"* and give up?

Mumia: Oh, no! Listen, I'm not just the busiest man on death row. I'm the busiest man I know. It ain't enough hours in a day. My days are very full. And there are a lot of projects that I can't even get to, even though I want to, because I'm so busy. How many dudes can say that?

Marc: Not many. But it's not just the amount of work you're doing, Mu. It's the purpose of the work. You're able to sustain yourself in the midst of absurdity because you're connected to something that's righteous and principled. Something bigger than you.

Mumia: Marc, the struggle against the death penalty is bigger than me. The struggle against the prison industrial complex is bigger than me. The struggle for social justice is bigger than me. And they will continue long after I'm gone. Struggle goes on. It's just important to know which side you're on.

Marc: Still, it must be tough to hold on to hope under these circumstances. Not to be grim, but your future hangs on a certain amount of faith in the system, the very system that you critique in your work as fundamentally unfair. To sustain hope in the face of that reality is pretty tough, no?

Mumia: Well I don't have faith or hope in the system. I haven't had that for many years. I have faith and hope in people. And, like I said, I don't waste time. If worse comes to worse then my time has still not been wasted. Dig what I'm sayin'? Because I know that my words are out there. Against all odds, I know that they're reaching people. I know this. I feel the vibration.

FOR YOUR LIBRARY

Live from Death Row **and** *Death Blossoms*, **Mumia Abu-Jamal**

The Prisoner's Wife, **asha bandele**

Soledad Brother, **George Jackson**

I Shall Not Die, **Billy Neal Moore**

Revolutionary Suicide, **Huey P. Newton**

The Cornel West Reader, **Cornel West**

ACKNOWLEDGEMENTS

Words are insufficient to express our gratitude to our editor, asha bandele. Through her multiple roles as critic, coach, comedian, psychologist, drill sergeant and Brooklyn Zionist, asha made this process more challenging, enlightening and loving than we could have ever imagined. A thousand thank you's.

Although her official title was "copy editor," Akiba Solomon was an indispensable part of this book's intellectual and creative development. Her brilliant insights and illuminating critiques pushed us far beyond what we thought were our intellectual limits. Merci mille fois!!!!!!

We are grateful to our creative director LaVon Leak, as well as photographer, Whitney Thomas, for transforming our fuzzy ideas into a beautiful final product.

We would like to thank our editorial assistant (and a brilliant scholar in her own right), Tara Conley, who spent countless hours transcribing our many conversations as well as offering indispensable early feedback. Without her work, this project quite literally may not have happened.

The incomparable Shunta Wilborn has provided invaluable assistance throughout every step of this process. From arranging prison visits to facilitating the editorial process, we have benefitted immeasurably from her loyalty, focus and attention to detail. We love you Tay Tay!

We send infinite love and gratitude to our friend, comrade and agent extraordinaire Frances Goldin, whose efforts allowed this book to be in your hands.

We are grateful for the unconditional support of Haki Madhubuti and Third World Press. For nearly 45 years, Haki has been a model of progressive thought, principled leadership, cooperative economics, institution building and grassroots activism. This book is a product of his remarkable vision and tireless commitment to Black people. We are honored and humbled to become part of the Third World Press tradition!

We are eternally grateful to countless comrades, colleagues, supporters, friends and family around the globe. Because of you, we have the strength to continue thinking, dreaming, loving, hoping and struggling for freedom.

By far, this has been the most collaborative book project that we've ever engaged. Through this process, we have been reminded of the boundless possibilities that exist when we commit to working, struggling and building together.

Let us continue to build…

Mumia Abu-Jamal

is an award-winning journalist and author who has spent the last 29 years on Pennsylvania's death row. His demand for a new trial and freedom is supported by heads of state, Nobel laureates, Amnesty International, the Congressional Black Caucus and other members of U.S. Congress and countless others who cherish justice, democracy and human rights. He is the author of six books, including *Live from Death Row, All Things Censored* and *Jailhouse Lawyers*.

You can write to Mumia at:

AM 8335

SCI-Greene

175 Progress Drive

Waynesburg, PA 15370

Marc Lamont Hill

is Associate Professor of Education at Teachers College, Columbia University. He also holds an affiliated faculty appointment in African-American Studies at the Institute for Research in African-American Studies at Columbia University. His work, which covers culture, politics and education, has appeared in numerous journals, magazines, books and anthologies. Dr. Hill has lectured widely and provides regular commentary for media outlets such as NPR, MSNBC and CNN. He is the host of the nationally syndicated television show, "Our World with Black Enterprise." Dr. Hill is the author of the award-winning book *Beats, Rhymes, and Classroom Life: Hip-Hop Pedagogy and the Politics of Identity* and a co-editor of *Media, Learning, and Sites of Possibility* and *The Anthropology of Education Reader.* **To contact Marc, please visit www.marclamonthill.com.**

CPSIA information can be obtained
at www.ICGtesting.com
Printed in the USA
LVHW081905121218
600076LV00043B/825/P